VEGAN HIGH-PROTEIN COOKBOOK FOR ATHLETES

2 BOOKS IN 1

High-Protein Delicious Recipes For A Plant-Based Diet Plan And Healthy Muscle In Bodybuilding, Fitness And Sports

Table of Contents
VEGAN COOKBOOK FOR ATHLETES

Description 9
INTRODUCTION TO THE VEGAN DIET 11
BREAKFAST RECIPES 12
1. Chocolate PB Smoothie 12
2. Orange french toast 13
3. Oatmeal Raisin Breakfast Cookie 14
4. Berry Beetsicle Smoothie 15
5. Blueberry Oat Muffins 16
6. Quinoa Applesauce Muffins 18
7. Blueberry Lemonade Smoothie 21
8. Berry Protein Smoothie 22
9. Green Kickstart Smoothie 24
10. Warm Maple and Cinnamon Quinoa 25
11. Warm Quinoa Breakfast Bowl 26
12. Banana Bread Rice Pudding 27
13. Mango Key Lime Pie Smoothie 29
14. Delicious Oat Meal 33
15. Breakfast Cherry Delight 34
16. Crazy Maple and Pear Breakfast 35
17. Hearty French Toast Bowls 36
18. Tofu Burrito 37
19. Tasty Mexican Breakfast 38
20. Divine Carrot Oatmeal 40
21. Wonderful Blueberry Butter 41
22. Delicious Pumpkin Butter 42
LUNCH RECIPES 43
23. Amazing Potato Dish 45
24. Textured Sweet Potatoes and Lentils Delight 46
25. Incredibly Tasty Pizza 47
26. Rich Beans Soup 49
27. Delicious Baked Beans 50
28. Indian Lentils 51
29. Delicious Butternut Squash Soup 52

- 30. Amazing Mushroom Stew 53
- 31. Simple Tofu Dish 54
- 32. Special Jambalaya 55
- 33. Delicious Chard Soup 56
- 34. Chinese Tofu and Veggies 57
- 35. Wonderful Corn Chowder 59
- 36. Black Eyed Peas Stew 60
- 37. White Bean Cassoulet 61
- 38. Light Jackfruit Dish 63
- 39. Veggie Curry 64

DINNER RECIPES 65
- 40. Low Carb Peanut Dip (Instant Pot) 65
- 41. Spice-Rubbed Cauliflower (Instant Pot) 67
- 42. Satay Veggie Bowl 67
- 43. Shiritaki Noodles and Veggies 69
- 44. Shiritaki Alfredo 70
- 45. Taco-Spiced Stir-fry 71
- 46. Green-Glory Soup (Instant Pot) 72
- 47. Mediterranean-Style Pasta 74
- 48. Kale-Stuffed Mushroom Caps 75
- 49. Boiled Seasoned Veggies (Instant Pot) 75
- 50. Cauliflower Soup (Instant Pot) 77
- 51. Tahini Covered Eggplant 78

DESSERT AND SNACK RECIPES 79
- 52. Banana-Nut Bread Bars 79
- 53. Lemon Coconut Cilantro Rolls 80
- 54. Tamari Almonds 81
- 55. Tempeh Taco Bites 82
- 56. Mushroom Croustades 84
- 57. Stuffed Cherry Tomatoes 85
- 58. Spicy Black Bean Dip 86
- 59. French Onion Pastry Puffs 87
- 60. Cheezy Cashew–Roasted Red Pepper Toasts 88
- 61. Baked Potato Chips 89
- 62. Mushrooms Stuffed With Spinach And Walnuts 91
- 63. Salsa Fresca 92

64. Guacamole 93
65. Veggie Hummus Pinwheels 94
66. Asian Lettuce Rolls 95
67. Pinto-Pecan Fireballs 96
68. Sweet Potato Biscuits 97
69. Lemon And Garlic Marinated Mushrooms 98
70. Garlic Toast 99
71. Vietnamese-Style Lettuce Rolls 100
72. Apple Crumble 101
73. Cashew-Chocolate Truffles 103
74. Banana Chocolate Cupcakes 104
75. Minty Fruit Salad 104
76. Mango Coconut Cream Pie 106
77. Cherry-Vanilla Rice Pudding (pressure cooker) 107
78. Mint Chocolate Chip Sorbet 108
79. Peach-Mango Crumble (pressure cooker) 109
80. Zesty Orange-Cranberry Energy Bites 110
81. Almond-Date Energy Bites 111
82. Chocolate Pudding 116
83. Coconut-Banana Pudding 118
84. Spiced Apple Chia Pudding 119
85. Salted Coconut-Almond Fudge 121
86. Caramelized Bananas 122
87. Peanut Butter Cups 124
88. Chocolate-Coconut Bars 126

SAUCES AND DIPS 127
89. Cucumber Bites 127
90. Broccoli Crispy Bread 127
91. Roasted Pumpkin Seeds 129
92. Multi Seeds Crackers 130
93. Almond Cauliflower 132
94. Tahini Dressing 133
95. Lemon & Mustard Vinaigrette 134
96. Cheesy Sauce 135
97. Chimichurri Style Sauce 136
98. Peanut Sauce 137

99.	Spicy Almond & Garlic Dip		138
100.	Cauliflower Hummus		139
101.	Eggplant & Walnut Spread		140
102.	Coconut Yogurt Dip		141
103.	Olive Tapenade		142
104.	Chunky Rocket Spread		143
CONCLUSION			144

Table of Contents
PLANT-BASED HIGH-PROTEIN COOKBOOK

Introduction.	146
What is plant-based diet?	147
8 ways to get started with a plant-based diet	149
Inspiration for plant-based eating throughout the day.	150
What plants are high in protein?	151
Why protein is important.	152
Soaking methods and cooking.	157
Seasoning	163
Testing for Doneness	165
Handy tips as a plant-based athlete.	172
Protein and recovery.	182
High protein salads.	219
Whole food dinners.	236
Snack and energy recovery.	256
Conclusion.	269

VEGAN COOKBOOK FOR ATHLETES

101 high-protein delicious recipes for a plant-based diet plan and For a Strong Body While Maintaining Health, Vitality and Energy

Description

As an athlete, it may sound like the vegan diet may not provide you the right Nutrition. But I am sure after reading these recipes; you can very well debunk that myth.

Inside this guide, there is a bunch of tasty and easy to cook recipes which will make sure that you get your share of protein and carbs. Remember that while being a meat free athlete ain't easy, this is hardly a reason to quit!

One of the greatest benefits of going vegan is the increased level of health you will experience and this manifests well beyond just your physique. Add to this the potent combination of healthy plant-based protein and you have a winner! You can also choose to supplement with vegan protein powder.

Remember to prep your meals ahead of time for maximum convenience. This guide covers the following recipes:
- Breakfast
- Lunch
- Dessert
- Desserts and snacks
- Sauces and dips

Happy Cooking!!

INTRODUCTION TO THE VEGAN DIET

A lot of people seeking to avoid a lifestyle that contributes to disorders and diseases such as heart attacks, type II diabetes and even cancer go Vegan. These people usually go vegan in order to reduce the intake of animal products and the harmful effects they can have on the body.

Most vegan products are plant based and they reduce the risk of these terrible diseases as well as lowering the risk of developing Alzheimer's disease and many others.

A Vegan diet also contributes to weight loss, not only is a plant-based diet less calorie dense, but provides the right nutrients to slim down quickly. A Vegan diet lowers cholesterol levels, LDLs and blood pressure - this will make you not only feel great, but look great too. In fact, people on a vegan diet typically have their blood pressure 25-75% lower than a person with an animal product diet. This also puts Vegans at a far lower risk of dementia.

Essentially, a Vegan diet will create a healthy lifestyle without even needing to work out. If you do work out as well though, that can produce some incredible results in terms of both weight loss and health! I will explore some of these benefits further later on in the book.

In addition, a lot of the antibiotics used in the modern animal farming system cause a lot of terrible side effects, and by going Vegan people are avoiding these.

For example, excess oestrogen, which is used in order to make animals more 'plump' to increase the meat industries 'yield', can contribute to weight gain when consumed by humans. In addition, high levels of oestrogen have been linked to gynecomastia (colloqually referred to as 'man boobs') in men.

BREAKFAST RECIPES
1. Chocolate PB Smoothie

Preparation time: 5 minutes
Cooking time: 0 minutes
Servings: 4
Ingredients
1 banana
¼ cup rolled oats, or 1 scoop plant protein powder
1 tablespoon flaxseed, or chia seeds
1 tablespoon unsweetened cocoa powder
1 tablespoon peanut butter, or almond or sunflower seed butter
1 tablespoon maple syrup (optional)
1 cup alfalfa sprouts, or spinach, chopped (optional)
½ cup non-dairy milk (optional)
1 cup water

Optional
1 teaspoon maca powder
1 teaspoon cocoa nibs

Directions
Purée everything in a blender until smooth, adding more water (or non-dairy milk) if needed. Add bonus boosters, as desired. Purée until blended.

Nutrition: calories: 474; protein: 13g; total fat: 16g; carbohydrates: 79g; fiber: 18g

2. Orange french toast

Preparation time: 15 minutes
Cooking time: 10 minutes
Servings: 4

Ingredients

3 very ripe bananas

1 cup unsweetened nondairy milk

Zest and juice of 1 orange

1 teaspoon ground cinnamon

¼ Teaspoon grated nutmeg

4 slices french bread

1 tablespoon coconut oil

Directions

In a blender, combine the bananas, almond milk, orange juice and zest, cinnamon, and nutmeg and blend until smooth. Pour the mixture into a 9-by-13-inch baking dish. Soak the bread in the mixture for 5 minutes on each side.

While the bread soaks, heat a griddle or sauté pan over medium-high heat. Melt the coconut oil in the pan and swirl to coat. Cook the bread slices until golden brown on both sides, about 5 minutes each. Serve immediately.

3. Oatmeal Raisin Breakfast Cookie

Preparation time: 5 minutes
Cooking time: 15 minutes

Servings: 2 cookies

Ingredients

½ Cup rolled oats

1 tablespoon whole-grain flour

½ Teaspoon baking powder

1 to 2 tablespoons brown sugar

½ Teaspoon pumpkin pie spice or ground cinnamon (optional)

¼ Cup unsweetened applesauce, plus more as needed

2 tablespoons raisins, dried cranberries, or vegan chocolate chips

Directions

In a medium bowl, stir together the oats, flour, baking powder, sugar, and pumpkin pie spice (if using). Stir in the applesauce until thoroughly combined. Add another 1 to 2 tablespoons of applesauce if the mixture looks too dry (this will depend on the type of oats used).

Shape the mixture into 2 cookies. Put them on a microwave-safe plate and heat on high power for 90 seconds. Alternatively, bake on a small tray in a 350°f oven or toaster oven for 15 minutes. Let cool slightly before eating.

Nutrition (2 cookies): calories: 175; protein: 74g; total fat: 2g; saturated fat:0g; carbohydrates: 39g; fiber: 4g

4. Berry Beetsicle Smoothie

Preparation time: 3 minutes
Cooking time: 0minutes
Servings: 1
Ingredients

½ Cup peeled and diced beets

½ Cup frozen raspberries

1 frozen banana

1 tablespoon maple syrup

1 cup unsweetened soy or almond milk

Directions

Combine all the Ingredients in a blender and blend until smooth.

5. Blueberry Oat Muffins

Preparation time: 10 minutes
Cooking time: 20 minutes
Servings: 12 mufins

Ingredients

2 tablespoons coconut oil or vegan margarine, melted, plus more for preparing the muffin tin

1 cup quick-cooking oats or instant oats

1 cup boiling water

½ Cup nondairy milk

¼ Cup ground flaxseed

1 teaspoon vanilla extract

1 teaspoon apple cider vinegar

1½ cups whole-grain flour

½ Cup brown sugar

2 teaspoons baking soda

Pinch salt

1 cup blueberries

Directions

Preheat the oven to 400°f.

Coat a muffin tin with coconut oil, line with paper muffin cups, or use a nonstick tin.

In a large bowl, combine the oats and boiling water. Stir so the oats soften. Add the coconut oil, milk, flaxseed, vanilla, and vinegar and stir to combine. Add the flour, sugar, baking soda, and salt. Stir until just combined. Gently fold in the blueberries. Scoop the muffin mixture into the prepared tin, about ⅓ cup for each muffin.

Bake for 20 to 25 minutes, until slightly browned on top and springy to the touch. Let cool for about 10 minutes. Run a dinner knife around the inside of each cup to loosen, then tilt the muffins on their sides in the muffin wells so air gets underneath. These keep in an airtight container in the refrigerator for up to 1 week or in the freezer indefinitely.

Nutrition (1muffin): calories: 174; protein: 5g; total fat: 3g; saturated fat:2g; carbohydrates: 33g; fiber: 4g

6. Quinoa Applesauce Muffins

Preparation time: 10 minutes
Cooking time: 15 minutes
Servings: 5

Ingredients

2 tablespoons coconut oil or margarine, melted, plus more for coating the muffin tin

¼ Cup ground flaxseed

½ Cup water

2 cups unsweetened applesauce

½ Cup brown sugar

1 teaspoon apple cider vinegar

2½ cups whole-grain flour

1½ cups cooked quinoa

2 teaspoons baking soda

Pinch salt

½ Cup dried cranberries or raisins

Directions

Preheat the oven to 400°f.

Coat a muffin tin with coconut oil, line with paper muffin cups, or use a nonstick tin. In a large bowl, stir together the flaxseed and water. Add the applesauce, sugar, coconut oil, and vinegar. Stir to combine. Add the flour, quinoa, baking soda, and salt, stirring until just combined. Gently fold in the cranberries without stirring too much. Scoop the muffin mixture into the prepared tin, about ⅓ cup for each muffin.

Bake for 15 to 20 minutes, until slightly browned on top and springy to the touch. Let cool for about 10 minutes. Run a dinner knife around the inside of each cup to loosen, then tilt the muffins on their sides in the muffin wells so air gets underneath. These keep in an airtight container in the refrigerator for up to 1 week or in the freezer indefinitely.

Per serving(1muffin): calories: 387; protein: 7g; total fat: 5g; saturated fat: 2g; carbohydrates: 57g; fiber: 8g

Pumpkin pancakes

Preparation time: 15 minutes
Cooking time: 15 minutes
Servings: 4

Ingredients

2 cups unsweetened almond milk

1 teaspoon apple cider vinegar

2½ cups whole-wheat flour

2 tablespoons baking powder

½ Teaspoon baking soda

1 teaspoon sea salt

1 teaspoon pumpkin pie spice or ½ teaspoon ground -cinnamon plus ¼ teaspoon grated -nutmeg plus ¼ teaspoon ground allspice

½ Cup canned pumpkin purée

1 cup water

1 tablespoon coconut oil

Directions

In a small bowl, combine the almond milk and apple cider vinegar. Set aside.

In a bowl, whisk together the flour, baking powder, baking soda, salt, and pumpkin pie spice. In bowl, combine the almond milk mixture, pumpkin purée, and water, whisking to mix well. Mix the wet Ingredients to the dry Ingredients and fold together until the dry -Ingredients are just moistened.

In a nonstick pan or griddle over medium-high heat, melt the coconut oil and swirl to coat. Pour the batter into the pan ¼ cup at a time and cook until the pancakes are browned, about 5 minutes per side. Serve immediately.

Green breakfast smoothie

Preparation time: 10 minutes
Cooking time: 0 minutes
Servings: 2

Ingredients

½ Banana, sliced

2 cups spinach or other greens, such as kale

1 cup sliced berries of your choosing, fresh or frozen

1 orange, peeled and cut into segments

1 cup unsweetened nondairy milk

1 cup ice

Directions

In a blender, combine all the Ingredients.

Starting with the blender on low speed, begin blending the smoothie, gradually increasing blender speed until smooth. Serve immediately.

7. Blueberry Lemonade Smoothie

Preparation time: 5 minutes
Cooking time: 0 minutes
Servings: 1
Ingredients
1 cup roughly chopped kale
¾ Cup frozen blueberries
1 cup unsweetened soy or almond milk
Juice of 1 lemon
1 tablespoon maple syrup

Directions

Combine all the Ingredients in a blender and blend until smooth. Enjoy immediately.

8. Berry Protein Smoothie

Preparation time: 5 minutes
Cooking time: 0 minutes
Servings: 1
Ingredients
1 banana
1 cup fresh or frozen berries
¾ Cup water or nondairy milk, plus more as needed
1 scoop plant-based protein powder, 3 ounces silken tofu, ¼ cup rolled oats, or ½ cup cooked quinoa

Additions
 1 tablespoon ground flaxseed or chia seeds
 1 handful fresh spinach or lettuce, or 1 chunk cucumber
Coconut water to replace some of the liquid

Directions:
In a blender, combine the banana, berries, water, and your choice of protein.

Add any addition **Ingredients** as desired. Purée until smooth and creamy, about 50 seconds.

Add a bit more water if you like a thinner smoothie.

Nutrition: calories: 332; protein: 7g; total fat: 5g; saturated fat: 1g; carbohydrates: 72g; fiber: 11g

Blueberry and chia smoothie

Preparation time: 10 minutes
Cooking time: 0 minutes
Servings: 2

Ingredients

2 tablespoons chia seeds

2 cups unsweetened nondairy milk

2 cups blueberries, fresh or frozen

2 tablespoons pure maple syrup or agave

2 tablespoons cocoa powder

Directions:

Soak the chia seeds in the almond milk for 5 minutes.

In a blender, combine the soaked chia seeds, almond milk, blueberries, maple syrup, and cocoa powder and blend until smooth. Serve immediately.

9. Green Kickstart Smoothie

Preparation time: 5 minutes
Cooking time: 0 minutes
Servings: 1

Ingredients

½ Avocado or 1 banana

½ Cup chopped cucumber, peeled if desired

1 handful fresh spinach or chopped lettuce

1 pear or apple, peeled and cored, or 1 cup unsweetened applesauce

2 tablespoons freshly squeezed lime juice

1 cup water or nondairy milk, plus more as needed

Additions

½-Inch piece peeled fresh ginger

1 tablespoon ground flaxseed or chia seeds

½ Cup soy yogurt or 3 ounces silken tofu

Coconut water to replace some of the liquid

2 tablespoons chopped fresh mint or ½ cup chopped mango

Directions:

In a blender, combine the avocado, cucumber, spinach, pear, lime juice, and water.

Add any Additions Ingredients as desired. Purée until smooth and creamy, about 50 seconds. Add a bit more water if you like a thinner smoothie.

Nutrition: calories: 263; protein: 4g; total fat: 14g; saturated fat: 2g; carbohydrates: 36g; fiber: 10g

10. Warm Maple and Cinnamon Quinoa

Preparation time: 5 minutes
Cooking time: 15 minutes
Servings: 4

Ingredients

1 cup unsweetened nondairy milk

1 cup water

1 cup quinoa, rinsed

1 teaspoon cinnamon

¼ Cup chopped pecans or other nuts or seeds, such as chia, sunflower seeds, or almonds

2 tablespoons pure maple syrup or agave

Directions:

In a medium saucepan over medium-high heat, bring the almond milk, water, and quinoa to a boil. Lower the heat to medium-low and cover. Simmer until the liquid is mostly absorbed and the quinoa softens, about 15 minutes.

Turn off the heat and allow to sit, covered, for 5 minutes. Stir in the cinnamon, pecans, and syrup. Serve hot.

11. Warm Quinoa Breakfast Bowl

Preparation time: 5 minutes
Cooking time: 0 minutes
Servings: 4

Ingredients

3 cups freshly cooked quinoa
1⅓ cups unsweetened soy or almond milk
2 bananas, sliced
1 cup raspberries
1 cup blueberries
½ Cup chopped raw walnuts
¼ Cup maple syrup

Directions:

Divide the Ingredients among 4 bowls, starting with a base of ¾ cup quinoa, ⅓ cup milk, ½ banana, ¼ cup raspberries, ¼ cup blueberries, and 2 tablespoons walnuts.

Drizzle 1 tablespoon of maple syrup over the top of each bowl.

12. Banana Bread Rice Pudding

Preparation time: 5 minutes
Cooking time: 50 minutes
Servings: 4

Ingredients

1 cup brown rice

1½ cups water

1½ cups nondairy milk

3 tablespoons sugar (omit if using a sweetened nondairy milk)

2 teaspoons pumpkin pie spice or ground cinnamon

2 bananas

3 tablespoons chopped walnuts or sunflower seeds (optional)

Directions

In a medium pot, combine the rice, water, milk, sugar, and pumpkin pie spice. Bring to a boil over high heat, turn the heat to low, and cover the pot. Simmer, stirring occasionally, until the rice is soft and the liquid is absorbed. White rice takes about 20 minutes; brown rice takes about 50 minutes.

Smash the bananas and stir them into the cooked rice. Serve topped with walnuts (if using). Leftovers will keep refrigerated in an airtight container for up to 5 days.

Nutrition: calories: 479; protein: 9g; total fat: 13g; saturated fat: 1g; carbohydrates: 86g; fiber: 7g

Apple and cinnamon oatmeal

Preparation time: 10 minutes
Cooking time: 10 minutes
Servings: 2

Ingredients

1¼ cups apple cider

1 apple, peeled, cored, and chopped

⅔ Cup rolled oats

1 teaspoon ground cinnamon

1 tablespoon pure maple syrup or agave (optional)

Directions

In a medium saucepan, bring the apple cider to a boil over medium-high heat. Stir in the apple, oats, and cinnamon.

Bring the cereal to a boil and turn down heat to low. Simmer until the oatmeal thickens, 3 to 4 minutes. Spoon into two bowls and sweeten with maple syrup, if using. Serve hot.

13. Mango Key Lime Pie Smoothie

Preparation time: 5 minutes
Cooking time: 0 minutes
Servings: 1
Ingredients

¼ Avocado

1 cup baby spinach

½ Cup frozen mango chunks

1 cup unsweetened soy or almond milk

Juice of 1 lime (preferably a key lime).

1 tablespoon maple syrup

Directions

Combine all the **Ingredients** in a blender and blend until smooth. Enjoy immediately.

Spiced orange breakfast couscous

Preparation time: 10 minutes
Cooking time: 10 minutes
Servings: 4

Ingredients

3 cups orange juice

1½ cups couscous

1 teaspoon ground cinnamon

¼ Teaspoon ground cloves

½ Cup dried fruit, such as raisins or apricots

½ Cup chopped almonds or other nuts or seeds

Directions

In a small saucepan, bring the orange juice to a boil. Add the couscous, cinnamon, and cloves and remove from heat. Cover the pan with a lid and allow to sit until the -couscous softens, about 5 minutes.

Fluff the couscous with a fork and stir in the dried fruit and nuts. Serve -immediately.

Breakfast parfaits

Preparation time: 15 minutes
Cooking time: 0 minutes
Servings: 2

Ingredients

One 14-ounce can coconut milk, refrigerated overnight

1 cup granola

½ Cup walnuts

1 cup sliced strawberries or other seasonal berries

Directions

Pour off the canned coconut-milk liquid and retain the solids.

In two parfait glasses, layer the coconut-milk solids, granola, walnuts, and -strawberries. Serve immediately.

Sweet potato and kale hash

Preparation time: 10 minutes
Cooking time: 15 minutes

Servings: 2

Ingredients

1 sweet potato

2 tablespoons olive oil

½ Onion, chopped

1 carrot, peeled and chopped

2 garlic cloves, minced

½ Teaspoon dried thyme

1 cup chopped kale

Sea salt

Freshly ground black pepper

Directions

Prick the sweet potato with a fork and microwave on high until soft, about 5 minutes. Remove from the microwave and cut into ¼-inch cubes.

In a large nonstick sauté pan, heat the olive oil over medium-high heat. Add the onion and carrot and cook until softened, about 5 minutes. Add the garlic and thyme and cook until the garlic is fragrant, about 30 seconds.

Add the sweet potatoes and cook until the potatoes begin to brown, about 7 -minutes. Add the kale and cook just until it wilts, 1 to 2 minutes. Season with salt and pepper. Serve immediately.

14. Delicious Oat Meal

Preparation time: 10 minutes
Cooking time: 6 hours
Servings: 4
Ingredients:
3 cups water
3 cups almond milk
1 and ½ cups steel oats
4 dates, pitted and chopped
1 teaspoon cinnamon, ground
2 tablespoons coconut sugar
½ Teaspoon ginger powder
A pinch of nutmeg, ground
A pinch of cloves, ground
1 teaspoon vanilla extract

Directions:
Put water and milk in your slow cooker and stir.
Add oats, dates, cinnamon, sugar, ginger, nutmeg, cloves and vanilla extract, stir, cover and cook on low for 6 hours.
Divide into bowls and serve for breakfast.

Enjoy!
Nutrition: calories 120, fat 1, fiber 2, carbs 3, protein 5

15. Breakfast Cherry Delight

Preparation time: 10 minutes
Cooking time: 8 hours and 10 minutes
Servings: 4
Ingredients:
2 cups almond milk
2 cups water
1 cup steel cut oats
2 tablespoons cocoa powder
1/3 cup cherries, pitted
¼ Cup maple syrup
½ Teaspoon almond extract

For the sauce:

2 tablespoons water
1 and ½ cups cherries, pitted and chopped
¼ Teaspoon almond extract

Directions:
Put the almond milk in your slow cooker.

Add 2 cups water, oats, cocoa powder, 1/3 cup cherries, maples syrup and ½ teaspoon almond extract.

Stir, cover and cook on low for 8 hours.

In a small pan, mix 2 tablespoons water with 1 and ½ cups cherries and ¼ teaspoon almond extract, stir well, bring to a simmer over medium heat and cook for 10 minutes until it thickens.

Divide oatmeal into breakfast bowls, top with the cherries sauce and serve.

Enjoy!
Nutrition: calories 150, fat 1, fiber 2, carbs 6, protein 5

16. Crazy Maple and Pear Breakfast

Preparation time: 10 minutes
Cooking time: 9 hours
Servings: 2
Ingredients:
1 pear, cored and chopped
½ Teaspoon maple extract
2 cups coconut milk
½ Cup steel cut oats
½ Teaspoon vanilla extract
1 tablespoon stevia
¼ Cup walnuts, chopped for serving
Cooking spray

Directions:
Spray your slow cooker with some cooking spray and add coconut milk.

Also, add maple extract, oats, pear, stevia and vanilla extract, stir, cover and cook on low for 9 hours.

Stir your oatmeal again, divide it into breakfast bowls and serve with chopped walnuts on top.

Enjoy!
Nutrition: calories 150, fat 3, fiber 2, carbs 6, protein 6

17. Hearty French Toast Bowls

Preparation time: 10 minutes
Cooking time: 5 hours
Servings: 4
Ingredients:
1 and ½ cups almond milk
1 cup coconut cream
1 tablespoon vanilla extract
½ Tablespoon cinnamon powder
2 tablespoons maple syrup
¼ Cup spenda
2 apples, cored and cubed
½ Cup cranberries, dried
1 pound vegan bread, cubed
Cooking spray

Directions:
Spray your slow cooker with some cooking spray and add the bread.
Also, add cranberries and apples and stir gently.
Add milk, coconut cream, maple syrup, vanilla extract, cinnamon powder and splenda.
Stir, cover and cook on low for 5 hours.
Divide into bowls and serve right away.

Enjoy!
Nutrition: calories 140, fat 2, fiber 3, carbs 6, protein 2

18. Tofu Burrito

Preparation time: 10 minutes
Cooking time: 8 hours
Servings: 4
Ingredients:
15 ounces canned black beans, drained
2 tablespoons onions, chopped
7 ounces tofu, drained and crumbled
2 tablespoons green bell pepper, chopped
½ Teaspoon turmeric
¾ Cup water
¼ Teaspoon smoked paprika
¼ Teaspoon cumin, ground
¼ Teaspoon chili powder
A pinch of salt and black pepper
4 gluten free whole wheat tortillas
Avocado, chopped for serving
Salsa for serving

Directions:
Put black beans in your slow cooker.
Add onions, tofu, bell pepper, turmeric, water, paprika, cumin, chili powder, a pinch of salt and pepper, stir, cover and cook on low for 8 hours.
Divide this on each tortilla, add avocado and salsa, wrap, arrange on plates and serve.

Enjoy!
Nutrition: calories 130, fat 4, fiber 2, carbs 5, protein 4

19. Tasty Mexican Breakfast

Preparation time: 10 minutes
Cooking time: 2 hours
Servings: 4
Ingredients:
1 cup brown rice
1 cup onion, chopped
2 cups veggie stock
1 red bell pepper, chopped
1 green bell pepper, chopped
4 ounces canned green chilies, chopped
15 ounces canned black beans, drained
A pinch of salt
Black pepper to the taste
For the salsa:
3 tablespoons lime juice
1 avocado, pitted, peeled and cubed
½ Cup cilantro, chopped
½ Cup green onions, chopped
½ Cup tomato, chopped
1 poblano pepper, chopped
2 tablespoons olive oil
½ Teaspoon cumin

Directions:
Put the stock in your slow cooker.
Add rice, onions and beans, stir, cover and cook on high for 1 hour and 30 minutes.

Add chilies, red and green bell peppers, a pinch of salt and black pepper, stir, cover again and cook on high for 30 minutes more.

Meanwhile, in a bowl, mix avocado with green onions, tomato, poblano pepper, cilantro, oil, cumin, a pinch of salt, black pepper and lime juice and stir really well.

Divide rice mix into bowls; top each with the salsa you've just made and serve.
Enjoy!
Nutrition: calories 140, fat 2, fiber 2, carbs 5, protein 5

20. Divine Carrot Oatmeal

Preparation time: 10 minutes
Cooking time: 7 hours
Servings: 3

Ingredients:

2 cups coconut milk
½ Cup old fashioned rolled oats
1 cup carrots, chopped
2 tablespoons agave nectar
1 teaspoon cardamom, ground
A pinch of saffron
Some chopped pistachios
Cooking spray

Directions:

Spray your slow cooker with some cooking spray and add coconut milk.

Also, add oats, carrots, agave nectar, cardamom and saffron.

Stir, cover and cook on Low for 7 hours.

Stir oatmeal again, divide into bowls and serve with chopped pistachios on top.

Enjoy!

Nutrition: calories 140, fat 2, fiber 2, carbs 4, protein 5

21. Wonderful Blueberry Butter

Preparation time: 10 minutes
Cooking time: 6 hours
Servings: 12
Ingredients:
5 cups blueberries puree
2 teaspoons cinnamon powder
Zest from 1 lemon
1 cup coconut sugar
½ Teaspoon nutmeg, ground
¼ Teaspoon ginger, ground

Directions:
Put blueberries in your slow cooker, cover and cook on low for 1 hour.

Stir your berries puree, cover and cook on low for 4 hours more.

Add sugar, ginger, nutmeg and lemon zest, stir and cook on high uncovered for 1 hour more.

Divide into jars, cover them and keep in a cold place until you serve it for breakfast.

Enjoy!
Nutrition: calories 143, fat 2, fiber 3, carbs 3, protein 4

22. Delicious Pumpkin Butter

Preparation time: 10 minutes
Cooking time: 4 hours
Servings: 5
Ingredients:
2 teaspoons cinnamon powder
4 cups pumpkin puree
1 and ¼ cup maple syrup
½ Teaspoon nutmeg
1 teaspoon vanilla extract
Directions:
In your slow cooker, mix pumpkin puree with maple syrup and vanilla extract, stir, cover and cook on high for 4 hours.

Add cinnamon and nutmeg, stir, divide into jars and serve for breakfast!
Enjoy!
Nutrition: calories 120, fat 2, fiber 2, carbs 4, protein 2

LUNCH RECIPES

Preparation time: 10 minutes
Cooking time: 3 hours
Servings: 4
Ingredients:
½ Cup quinoa
2 and ½ cups veggie stock
14 ounces canned tomatoes, chopped
15 ounces canned black beans, drained
¼ Cup green bell pepper, chopped
¼ Cup red bell pepper, chopped
A pinch of salt and black pepper
2 garlic cloves, minced
1 carrots, shredded
1 small chili pepper, chopped
2 teaspoons chili powder
1 teaspoon cumin, ground
A pinch of cayenne pepper
½ Cup corn
1 teaspoon oregano, dried
<u>For the vegan sour cream:</u>
A drizzle of apple cider vinegar
4 tablespoons water
½ Cup cashews, soaked overnight and drained
1 teaspoon lime juice

Directions:
Put the stock in your slow cooker.
Add quinoa, tomatoes, beans, red and green bell pepper, garlic, carrot, salt, pepper, corn, cumin, cayenne, chili powder, chili pepper and oregano, stir, cover and cook on High for 3 hours.
Meanwhile, put the cashews in your blender.
Add water, vinegar and lime juice and pulse really well.

Divide beans chili into bowls, top with vegan sour cream and serve.

Enjoy!

Nutrition: calories 300, fat 4, fiber 4, carbs 10, protein 7

23. Amazing Potato Dish

Preparation time: 10 minutes
Cooking time: 3 hours
Servings: 4
Ingredients:
1 and ½ pounds potatoes, peeled and roughly chopped
1 tablespoon olive oil
3 tablespoons water
1 small yellow onion, chopped
½ Cup veggie stock cube, crumbled
½ Teaspoon coriander, ground
½ Teaspoon cumin, ground
½ Teaspoon garam masala
½ Teaspoon chili powder
Black pepper to the taste
½ Pound spinach, roughly torn

Directions:
Put the potatoes in your slow cooker.
Add oil, water, onion, stock cube, coriander, cumin, garam masala, chili powder, black pepper and spinach.
Stir, cover and cook on High for 3 hours.
Divide into bowls and serve.

Enjoy!
Nutrition: calories 270, fat 4, fiber 6, carbs 8, protein 12

24. Textured Sweet Potatoes and Lentils Delight

Preparation time: 10 minutes
Cooking time: 4 hours and 30 minutes
Servings: 6
Ingredients:

6 cups sweet potatoes, peeled and cubed
2 teaspoons coriander, ground
2 teaspoons chili powder
1 yellow onion, chopped
3 cups veggie stock
4 garlic cloves, minced
A pinch of sea salt and black pepper
10 ounces canned coconut milk
1 cup water
1 and ½ cups red lentils

Directions:

Put sweet potatoes in your slow cooker.

Add coriander, chili powder, onion, stock, garlic, salt and pepper, stir, cover and cook on high for 3 hours.

Add lentils, stir, cover and cook for 1 hour and 30 minutes.

Add water and coconut milk, stir well, divide into bowls and serve right away.

Enjoy!

Nutrition: calories 300, fat 10, fiber 8, carbs 16, protein 10

25. Incredibly Tasty Pizza

Preparation time: 1 hour and 10 minutes
Cooking time: 1 hour and 45 minutes
Servings: 3
Ingredients:
For the dough:
½ Teaspoon italian seasoning
1 and ½ cups whole wheat flour
1 and ½ teaspoons instant yeast
1 tablespoon olive oil
A pinch of salt
½ Cup warm water
Cooking spray
For the sauce:
¼ Cup green olives, pitted and sliced
¼ Cup kalamata olives, pitted and sliced
½ Cup tomatoes, crushed
1 tablespoon parsley, chopped
1 tablespoon capers, rinsed
¼ Teaspoon garlic powder
¼ Teaspoon basil, dried
¼ Teaspoon oregano, dried
¼ Teaspoon palm sugar
¼ Teaspoon red pepper flakes
A pinch of salt and black pepper
½ Cup cashew mozzarella, shredded

Directions:

In your food processor, mix yeast with italian seasoning, a pinch of salt and flour.

Add oil and the water and blend well until you obtain a dough.

Transfer dough to a floured working surface, knead well, transfer to a greased bowl, cover and leave aside for 1 hour.

Meanwhile, in a bowl, mix green olives with kalamata olives, tomatoes, parsley, capers, garlic powder, oregano, sugar, salt, pepper and pepper flakes and stir well.

Transfer pizza dough to a working surface again and flatten it.

Shape so it will fit your slow cooker.

Grease your slow cooker with cooking spray and add dough.

Press well on the bottom.

Spread the sauce mix all over, cover and cook on high for 1 hour and 15 minutes.

Spread vegan mozzarella all over, cover again and cook on high for 30 minutes more.

Leave your pizza to cool down before slicing and serving it.

Nutrition: calories 340, fat 5, fiber 7, carbs 13, protein 15

26. Rich Beans Soup

Preparation time: 10 minutes
Cooking time: 7 hours
Servings: 4
Ingredients:
1 pound navy beans
1 yellow onion, chopped
4 garlic cloves, crushed
2 quarts veggie stock
A pinch of sea salt
Black pepper to the taste
2 potatoes, peeled and cubed
2 teaspoons dill, dried
1 cup sun-dried tomatoes, chopped
1 pound carrots, sliced
4 tablespoons parsley, minced

Directions:
Put the stock in your slow cooker.
Add beans, onion, garlic, potatoes, tomatoes, carrots, dill, salt and pepper, stir, cover and cook on low for 7 hours.
Stir your soup, add parsley, divide into bowls and serve.
Enjoy!
Nutrition: calories 250, fat 4, fiber 3, carbs 9, protein 10

27. Delicious Baked Beans

Preparation time: 10 minutes
Cooking time: 12 hours
Servings: 8
Ingredients:
1 pound navy beans, soaked overnight and drained
1 cup maple syrup
1 cup bourbon
1 cup vegan bbq sauce
1 cup palm sugar
¼ Cup ketchup
1 cup water
¼ Cup mustard
¼ Cup blackstrap molasses
¼ Cup apple cider vinegar
¼ Cup olive oil
2 tablespoons coconut aminos

Directions:
Put the beans in your slow cooker.
Add maple syrup, bourbon, bbq sauce, sugar, ketchup, water, mustard, molasses, vinegar, oil and coconut aminos.
Stir everything, cover and cook on Low for 12 hours.
Divide into bowls and serve.

Enjoy!
Nutrition: calories 430, fat 7, fiber 8, carbs 15, protein 19

28. Indian Lentils

Preparation time: 10 minutes
Cooking time: 3 hours
Servings: 4
Ingredients:
1 yellow bell pepper, chopped
1 sweet potato, chopped
2 and ½ cups lentils, already cooked
4 garlic cloves, minced
1 yellow onion, chopped
2 teaspoons cumin, ground
15 ounces canned tomato sauce
½ Teaspoon ginger, ground
A pinch of cayenne pepper
1 tablespoons coriander, ground
1 teaspoon turmeric, ground
2 teaspoons paprika
2/3 cup veggie stock
1 teaspoon garam masala
A pinch of sea salt
Black pepper to the taste
Juice of 1 lemon

Directions:
Put the stock in your slow cooker.
Add potato, lentils, onion, garlic, cumin, bell pepper, tomato sauce, salt, pepper, ginger, coriander, turmeric, paprika, cayenne, garam masala and lemon juice.
Stir, cover and cook on high for 3 hours.
Stir your lentils mix again, divide into bowls and serve.

Enjoy!
Nutrition: calories 300, fat 6, fiber 5, carbs 9, protein 12

29. Delicious Butternut Squash Soup

Preparation time: 10 minutes
Cooking time: 6 hours
Servings: 8
Ingredients:
1 apple, cored, peeled and chopped
½ Pound carrots, chopped
1 pound butternut squash, peeled and cubed
1 yellow onion, chopped
A pinch of sea salt
Black pepper to the taste
1 bay leaf
3 cups veggie stock
14 ounces canned coconut milk
¼ Teaspoon sage, dried

Directions:
Put the stock in your slow cooker.
Add apple squash, carrots, onion, salt, pepper and bay leaf.
Stir, cover and cook on low for 6 hours.
Transfer to your blender, add coconut milk and sage and pulse really well.
Ladle into bowls and serve right away.

Enjoy!
Nutrition: calories 200, fat 3, fiber 6, carbs 8, protein 10

30. Amazing Mushroom Stew

Preparation time: 10 minutes
Cooking time: 8 hours
Servings: 4
Ingredients:
2 garlic cloves, minced
1 celery stalk, chopped
1 yellow onion, chopped
1 and ½ cups firm tofu, pressed and cubed
1 cup water
10 ounces mushrooms, chopped
1 pound mixed peas, corn and carrots
2 and ½ cups veggie stock
1 teaspoon thyme, dried
2 tablespoons coconut flour
A pinch of sea salt
Black pepper to the taste

Directions:
Put the water and stock in your slow cooker.
Add garlic, onion, celery, mushrooms, mixed veggies, tofu, thyme, salt, pepper and flour.
Stir everything, cover and cook on low for 8 hours.
Divide into bowls and serve hot.

Enjoy!
Nutrition: calories 230, fat 4, fiber 6, carbs 10, protein 7

31. Simple Tofu Dish

Preparation time: 10 minutes
Cooking time: 3 hours
Servings: 6
Ingredients:
1 big tofu package, cubed
1 tablespoon sesame oil
¼ Cup pineapple, cubed
1 tablespoon olive oil
2 garlic cloves, minced
1 tablespoons brown rice vinegar
2 teaspoon ginger, grated
¼ Cup soy sauce
5 big zucchinis, cubed
¼ Cup sesame seeds

Directions:
In your food processor, mix sesame oil with pineapple, olive oil, garlic, ginger, soy sauce and vinegar and whisk well.

Add this to your slow cooker and mix with tofu cubes.

Cover and cook on High for 2 hours and 45 minutes.

Add sesame seeds and zucchinis, stir gently, cover and cook on High for 15 minutes.

Divide between plates and serve.

Enjoy!

Nutrition: calories 200, fat 3, fiber 4, carbs 9, protein 10

32. Special Jambalaya

Preparation time: 10 minutes
Cooking time: 6 hours
Servings: 4
Ingredients:
6 ounces soy chorizo, chopped
1 and ½ cups celery ribs, chopped
1 cup okra
1 green bell pepper, chopped
16 ounces canned tomatoes and green chilies, chopped
2 garlic cloves, minced
½ Teaspoon paprika
1 and ½ cups veggie stock
A pinch of cayenne pepper
Black pepper to the taste
A pinch of salt
3 cups already cooked wild rice for serving

Directions:
Heat up a pan over medium high heat, add soy chorizo, stir, brown for a few minutes and transfer to your slow cooker.

Also, add celery, bell pepper, okra, tomatoes and chilies, garlic, paprika, salt, pepper and cayenne to your slow cooker.

Stir everything, add veggie stock, cover the slow cooker and cook on low for 6 hours.

Divide rice on plates, top each serving with your vegan jambalaya and serve hot.

Enjoy!
Nutrition: calories 150, fat 3, fiber 7, carbs 15, protein 9

33. Delicious Chard Soup

Preparation time: 10 minutes
Cooking time: 8 hours
Servings: 6
Ingredients:
1 yellow onion, chopped
1 tablespoon olive oil
1 celery stalk, chopped
2 garlic cloves, minced
1 carrot, chopped
1 bunch swiss chard, torn
1 cup brown lentils, dried
5 potatoes, peeled and cubed
1 tablespoon soy sauce
Black pepper to the taste
A pinch of sea salt
6 cups veggie stock

Directions:
Heat up a big pan with the oil over medium high heat, add onion, celery, garlic, carrot and Swiss chard, stir, cook for a few minutes and transfer to your slow cooker.

Also, add lentils, potatoes, soy sauce, salt, pepper and stock to the slow cooker, stir, cover and cook on Low for 8 hours.

Divide into bowls and serve hot.

Enjoy!

Nutrition: calories 200, fat 4, fiber 5, carbs 9, protein 12

34. Chinese Tofu and Veggies

Preparation time: 10 minutes
Cooking time: 4 hours
Servings: 4
Ingredients:
14 ounces extra firm tofu, pressed and cut into medium triangles
Cooking spray
2 teaspoons ginger, grated
1 yellow onion, chopped
3 garlic cloves, minced
8 ounces tomato sauce
¼ Cup hoisin sauce
¼ Teaspoon coconut aminos
2 tablespoons rice wine vinegar
1 tablespoon soy sauce
1 tablespoon spicy mustard
¼ Teaspoon red pepper, crushed
2 teaspoons molasses
2 tablespoons water
A pinch of black pepper
3 broccoli stalks
1 green bell pepper, cut into squares
2 zucchinis, cubed

Directions:
Heat up a pan over medium high heat, add tofu pieces, brown them for a few minutes and transfer to your slow cooker.

Heat up the pan again over medium high heat, add ginger, onion, garlic and tomato sauce, stir, sauté for a few minutes and transfer to your slow cooker as well.

Add hoisin sauce, aminos, vinegar, soy sauce, mustard, red pepper, molasses, water and black pepper, stir gently, cover and cook on high for 3 hours.

Add zucchinis, bell pepper and broccoli, cover and cook on high for 1 more hour.

Divide between plates and serve right away.

Enjoy!

Nutrition: calories 300, fat 4, fiber 8, carbs 14, protein 13

35. Wonderful Corn Chowder

Preparation time: 10 minutes
Cooking time: 8 hours and 30 minutes
Servings: 6
Ingredients:
2 cups yellow onion, chopped
2 tablespoons olive oil
1 red bell pepper, chopped
1 pound gold potatoes, cubed
1 teaspoon cumin, ground
4 cups corn kernels
4 cups veggie stock
1 cup almond milk
A pinch of salt
A pinch of cayenne pepper
½ Teaspoon smoked paprika
Chopped scallions for serving

Directions:
Heat up a pan with the oil over medium heat, add onion, stir and sauté for 5 minutes and then transfer to your slow cooker.
Add bell pepper, 1 cup corn, potatoes, paprika, cumin, salt and cayenne, stir, cover and cook on low for 8 hours.
Blend this using an immersion blender and then mix with almond milk and the rest of the corn.
Stir chowder, cover and cook on low for 30 minutes more.
Ladle into bowls and serve with chopped scallions on top.

Enjoy!
Nutrition: calories 200, fat 4, fiber 7, carbs 13, protein 16

36. Black Eyed Peas Stew

Preparation time: 10 minutes
Cooking time: 4 hours
Servings: 8
Ingredients:
3 celery stalks, chopped
2 carrots, sliced
1 yellow onion, chopped
1 sweet potato, cubed
1 green bell pepper, chopped
3 cups black-eyed peas, soaked for 8 hours and drained
1 cup tomato puree
4 cups veggie stock
A pinch of salt
Black pepper to the taste
1 chipotle chile, minced
1 teaspoon ancho chili powder
1 teaspoons sage, dried and crumbled
2 teaspoons cumin, ground
Chopped coriander for serving

Directions:
Put celery in your slow cooker.
Add carrots, onion, potato, bell pepper, black-eyed peas, tomato puree, salt, pepper, chili powder, sage, chili, cumin and stock.
Stir, cover and cook on High for 4 hours.
Stir stew again, divide into bowls and serve with chopped coriander on top.
Enjoy!
Nutrition: calories 200, fat 4, fiber 7, carbs 9, protein 16

37. White Bean Cassoulet

Preparation time: 10 minutes
Cooking time: 6 hours
Servings: 4
Ingredients:
2 celery stalks, chopped
3 leeks, sliced
4 garlic cloves, minced
2 carrots, chopped
2 cups veggie stock
15 ounces canned tomatoes, chopped
1 bay leaf
1 tablespoon italian seasoning
30 ounces canned white beans, drained

For the breadcrumbs:
Zest from 1 lemon, grated
1 garlic clove, minced
2 tablespoons olive oil
1 cup vegan bread crumbs
¼ Cup parsley, chopped

Directions:
Heat up a pan with a splash of the veggie stock over medium heat, add celery and leeks, stir and cook for 2 minutes.

Add carrots and garlic, stir and cook for 1 minute more.

Add this to your slow cooker and mix with stock, tomatoes, bay leaf, italian seasoning and beans.

Stir, cover and cook on low for 6 hours.

Meanwhile, heat up a pan with the oil over medium high heat, add bread crumbs, lemon zest, 1 garlic clove and parsley, stir and toast for a couple of minutes.

Divide your white beans mix into bowls, sprinkle bread crumbs mix on top and serve.

Enjoy!
Nutrition: calories 223, fat 3, fiber 7, carbs 10, protein 7

38. Light Jackfruit Dish

Preparation time: 10 minutes
Cooking time: 6 hours
Servings: 4
Ingredients:
40 ounces green jackfruit in brine, drained
½ Cup agave nectar
½ Cup gluten free tamari sauce
¼ Cup soy sauce
1 cup white wine
2 tablespoons ginger, grated
8 garlic cloves, minced
1 pear, cored and chopped
1 yellow onion, chopped
½ Cup water
4 tablespoons sesame oil

Directions:
Put jackfruit in your slow cooker.
Add agave nectar, tamari sauce, soy sauce, wine, ginger, garlic, pear, onion, water and oil.
Stir well, cover and cook on low for 6 hours.
Divide jackfruit mix into bowls and serve.
Enjoy!
Nutrition: calories 160, fat 4, fiber 1, carbs 10, protein 3

39. Veggie Curry

Preparation time: 10 minutes
Cooking time: 4 hours
Servings: 4
Ingredients:
1 tablespoon ginger, grated
14 ounces canned coconut milk
Cooking spray
16 ounces firm tofu, pressed and cubed
1 cup veggie stock
¼ Cup green curry paste
½ Teaspoon turmeric
1 tablespoon coconut sugar
1 yellow onion, chopped
1 and ½ cup red bell pepper, chopped
A pinch of salt
¾ Cup peas
1 eggplant, chopped

Directions:
Put the coconut milk in your slow cooker.
Add ginger, stock, curry paste, turmeric, sugar, onion, bell pepper, salt, peas and eggplant pieces, stir, cover and cook on high for 4 hours.
Meanwhile, spray a pan with cooking spray and heat up over medium high heat.
Add tofu pieces and brown them for a few minutes on each side.
Divide tofu into bowls, add slowly cooked curry mix on top and serve.
Enjoy!
Nutrition: calories 200, fat 4, fiber 6, carbs 10, protein 9

DINNER RECIPES
40. Low Carb Peanut Dip (Instant Pot)

Servings: 6
Preparation time: 10 minutes
Nutrition
Calories: 451 kcal

Carbs: 18.9g

Fat: 37.7g

Protein: 9.8g

Fiber: 4.9g

Sugar: 3.7g

Ingredients:

2 tbsp. Peanut oil

1 cup peanut cheese spread

1 low carb crust

1 cup onion (chopped)

1 tbsp. Garlic (minced)

1 cup fire roasted tomatoes

1 tbsp. Chipotle pepper (chopped)

½ Cup water

1 tbsp. Chili powder

2 tsp. Ground cumin

2 tsp. Salt

1 tsp. Dried oregano

Total number of **Ingredients**: 12

Directions:

Select the "sauté" option on the instant pot, waiting till it reads "hot" to add the onions and garlic with olive oil, stirring for about 30 minutes.

Blend the canned tomatoes and the peanut butter until it is relatively smooth.

Mix the cumin, salt, chili powder, and oregano; then mix with the onions and garlic for 30 seconds, allowing them to soak in the flavor.

Pour the blender mix into the pot along with the water. Close the pot and cook on instant pressure for 10 minutes, allowing natural pressure release for 10 minutes after that.

Mix well, and serve with a low carb crust for dipping!

41. Spice-Rubbed Cauliflower (Instant Pot)

Servings: 4
Preparation time: 10 minutes
Nutrition
Calories: 86 kcal

Carbs: 12.3g

Fat: 2.7g

Protein: 3.3g

Fiber: 7.5g

Sugar: 5.6g

Ingredients:

2 lbs. Cauliflower

2 tbsp. Olive oil

2 tsp. Paprika

2 tsp. Ground cumin

Salt to taste

1 cup cilantro (fresh, chopped)

1 lemon (quartered)

Total number of **Ingredients**: 7

Directions:

Insert the steam rack in the instant pot, adding 1 ½ cups of water.

Remove the leaves of the cauliflower, cut the end from the base, and place on the steam rack.

Combine the oil, salt, paprika, and cumin in a bowl; then pour over the cauliflower to coat.

Lock the lid and cook under pressure for 4 minutes; use the quick release to let out the steam, and open the lid.

Take the cauliflower out and cut it into 1 inch sized "steaks."

Divide onto plates, sprinkle the cilantro on top, and place a quartered lemon on each plate.

42. Satay Veggie Bowl

Servings: 4
Preparation time: 15 minutes

Nutrition

Calories: 605 kcal

Carbs: 16g

Fat: 53.1g

Protein: 15.9g

Fiber: 9.8g

Sugar: 4.7g

Ingredients:

Handful of olives

Olive oil, garlic powder, and salt to taste

1 cup broccoli (florets)

1 cup spinach (frozen)

3 cups peanut butter or cashew cheese

Total number of **Ingredients:** 5

Directions:

In a greased skillet, add broccoli, and frozen spinach.

Adding salt and garlic powder to taste, mix well and wait until the spinach has softened and the tempeh is cooked.

Transfer to a bowl, and add olive oil, garlic powder, and salt to taste. Garnish with olives.

43. Shiritaki Noodles and Veggies

Servings: 1
Preparation time: 15 minutes

Nutrition

Calories: 279 kcal

Carbs: 13.5g

Fat: 28.2g

Protein: 3.0g

Fiber: 4.6g

Sugar: 5.2g

Ingredients:

1 package shiritaki noodles (rinsed, drained)

2 tbsp. Peanut oil

¼ Cup marinara sauce

½ Cup mixed veggies (of choice)

Total number of **Ingredients:** 4

Directions:

Boil the noodles until soft.

Once done, transfer to a skillet and add the marinara sauce, oil, and mixed veggies.

Keep mixing, letting the mixture heat until the veggies are warm and incorporated.

44. Shiritaki Alfredo

Servings: 1
Preparation time: 10 minutes
Nutrition
Calories: 377 kcal
Carbs: 11.3g
Fat: 34.3g
Protein: 5.6g
Fiber: 5.5g
Sugar: 1.0g

Ingredients:

1 package shiritaki noodles (rinsed, drained)
2 tbsp. Olive oil
¼ Cup vegan cream cheese
1 cup spinach (frozen)
Salt, pepper, and garlic powder (to taste)
Almond milk (to reach desired consistency)
Total number of **Ingredients:** 8

Directions:

Dump all Ingredients in a pan with olive oil and slowly add almond milk for a creamy feel.

Once all Ingredients are mixed and the milk thickens, turn off the heat and serve.

45. Taco-Spiced Stir-fry

Servings: 1
Preparation time: 15 minutes

Nutrition

Calories: 293 kcal

Carbs: 18.7g

Fat: 22.5g

Protein: 4.0g

Fiber: 10.5g

Sugar: 3.7g

Ingredients:

1 package cauliflower rice

1 tbsp. Peanut oil

1 tbsp. Taco seasoning

½ Tbsp. Chili powder

2 tbsp. Guacamole

¼ Cup sliced olives

Total number of **Ingredients:** 6

Directions:

Mix all Ingredients, except the guacamole and olives, in a pan on medium heat until the cauliflower rice has softened.

Take off the stove and it cool when rice has softened, before serving.

46. Green-Glory Soup (Instant Pot)

Servings: 6
Preparation time: 15 minutes
Nutrition
Calories: 284 kcal
Carbs: 9.1g
Fat: 26.3g
Protein: 2.9g
Fiber: 3.1g
Sugar: 5.3g

Ingredients:
1 head cauliflower (florets)
1 onion (diced)
2 cloves garlic (minced)
1 cup spinach (fresh or frozen)
1 bay leaf (crumbled)
1 cup coconut milk
4 cups vegetable stock
Salt and pepper to taste
Herbs for garnish (optional)
½ Cup coconut oil
Total number of **Ingredients:** 11

Directions:
In a pressure pot on "sauté" mode, sauté onions and garlic until onions are browned. Once cooked, add the cauliflower and bay leaf and cook for about 5 minutes, stirring occasionally.

Add the spinach and continue cooking and stirring for 5 minutes.

Pour in the vegetable stock and set the timer for 10 minutes on high pressure to let the mix come to a boil; then allow quick pressure release and add the coconut milk.

Season with garnishes of choice as well as salt and pepper. Turn off the pot and mix the soup until it becomes thick and creamy with a hand blender.

47. Mediterranean-Style Pasta

Servings: 4
Preparation time: 10 minutes
Nutrition

Calories: 117 kcal

Carbs: 7.9g

Fat: 8.7g

Protein: 1.8g

Fiber: 2.6g

Sugar: 4.2g

Ingredients:

2 zucchinis (large, spiral-sliced)

1 cup spinach

2 tbsp. Olive oil

5 cloves garlic (minced)

Salt and pepper (to taste)

¼ Cup tomatoes (sun dried for added flavor)

2 tbsp. Capers

2 tbsp. Parsley (chopped)

10 kalamata olives (halved)

Total number of **Ingredients:** 10

Directions:

In a lightly oiled pan, add the spinach, zucchini, salt, pepper, and garlic, sautéing until the zucchini is tender; drain the excess liquid.

Add tomatoes, capers, olives, and parsley, mixing for about 3 minutes.

Remove from heat and toss well before serving, adding more or less of any item for preference.

48. Kale-Stuffed Mushroom Caps

Servings: 2
Preparation time: 15 minutes
Nutrition
Calories: 81 kcal
Carbs: 7.3g
Fat: 4.8g
Protein: 3g
Fiber: 2.2g
Sugar: 1.1g

Ingredients:
4 cups kale (fresh, chopped)
2 tbsp. Olive oil
3 tsp. Garlic (minced)
1 tsp. Garlic powder
½ Tsp. Salt
4 portobello mushroom caps (large)
Total number of **Ingredients:** 6

Directions:
Sauté the garlic and olive oil in a pan. Before it burns, add the kale, stirring well for about 7 minutes. Then add the garlic powder and salt, stirring well for 3 more minutes. Turn off the heat.

Mix the other half of the olive oil and garlic, then rub on the mushroom caps.

Place caps on the grill on medium heat, allowing them to cook for about 10 minutes—5 minutes per side—until tender.

Remove from the grill and divide your kale mixture on top of each cap; serve and enjoy.

Check out this recipe for a delicious, unique treat to spice up any dinner or gathering.

49. Boiled Seasoned Veggies (Instant Pot)

Servings: 1
Preparation time: 15 minutes
Nutrition
Calories: 816 kcal
Carbs: 66.1g
Fat: 55.8g
Protein: 12.5g
Fiber: 26.9g
Sugar: 32.2g

Ingredients:
1 eggplant (cubed, medium)
2 zucchinis (halved and sliced)
8 oz. Mushrooms (of choice, quartered)
6 cloves garlic (minced)
3 sprigs fresh rosemary (chopped)
¼ Cup olive oil
2 tbsp. Balsamic vinegar
2 tbsp. Dried onion flakes
½ Cup water
Salt and pepper to taste
Total number of **Ingredients:** 11

Directions:
Preheat oven to 400°f.

In a bowl, mix all Ingredients, lightly tossing and making sure all the vegetables are coated in spices and olive oil.

Throw mixture in a pressure pot with ½ cup of water and cook on high pressure for about 20 minutes, allowing for natural pressure release once time is up.

Open, and add more or less of the spices you prefer.

If you're a veggie lover, you are sure to love this dish. Vegetables are heart-healthy, filling, and kind alternatives to other non-vegan or ketogenic meals!

50. Cauliflower Soup (Instant Pot)

Servings: 6
Preparation time: 10 minutes

Nutrition

Calories: 43 kcal

Carbs: 4.3g

Fat: 2.2g

Protein: 1.4g

Fiber: 1.3g

Sugar: 2.2g

Ingredients:

3 cups vegetable stock

2 tsp. Thyme powder

½ Tsp. Matcha green tea powder

1 head cauliflower (about 2.5 cups, florets)

1 tbsp. Olive oil

5 garlic cloves (minced)

Salt and pepper to taste

Total number of **Ingredients:** 8

Directions:

In an instant pressure pot, add the vegetable stock, thyme, and matcha powder on medium heat. Bring to a boil.

Add the cauliflower and set timer for 10 minutes on high pressure, allowing for quick pressure release when finished.

In a saucepan, add garlic and olive oil until tender, and you can smell it; then add it to the pot along with salt and cook for 1 to 2 minutes.

Turn off the heat and. Blend the soup until smooth and creamy with a blender.

51. Tahini Covered Eggplant

Servings: 1
Preparation time: 20 minutes
Nutrition
Calories: 474 kcal
Carbs: 41.9g
Fat: 31.2g
Protein: 6.3g
Fiber: 21.9g
Sugar: 17.9g

Ingredients:
1 eggplant (sliced)
1 garlic clove (minced)
1 tbsp. Olive oil
Salt and pepper (to taste)
½ Cup chopped parsley
Sauce:
1 tsp. Olive oil
1 onion (chopped)
½ Garlic clove (chopped)
Handful of parsley (chopped)
⅓ Cup almond milk
1 tsp. Tahini
Salt (to taste)
Total number of **Ingredients:** 12

Directions:
Preheat oven to 350°f.
Mix all Ingredients in a medium bowl with the eggplant.
Place on baking tray, and bake for 30 minutes.
Sauce:
Blend all Ingredients. Add more or less to taste.

DESSERT AND SNACK RECIPES

52. Banana-Nut Bread Bars

Preparation time: 5 minutes
Cooking time: 30 minutes
Servings: 9 bars

Ingredients

Nonstick cooking spray (optional)

2 large ripe bananas

1 tablespoon maple syrup

½ Teaspoon vanilla extract

2 cups old-fashioned rolled oats

½ Teaspoons salt

¼ Cup chopped walnuts

Directions:

Preheat the oven to 350ºf. Lightly coat a 9-by-9-inch baking pan with nonstick cooking spray (if using) or line with parchment paper for oil-free baking.

In a medium bowl, mash the bananas with a fork. Add the maple syrup and vanilla extract and mix well. Add the oats, salt, and walnuts, mixing well.

Transfer the batter to the baking pan and bake for 25 to 30 minutes, until the top is crispy. Cool completely before slicing into 9 bars. Transfer to an airtight storage container or a large plastic bag.

Nutrition (1 bar): calories: 73; fat: 1g; protein: 2g; carbohydrates: 15g; fiber: 2g; sugar: 5g; sodium: 129mg

53. Lemon Coconut Cilantro Rolls

Preparation time: 30 minutes • chill time: 30 minutes
Servings: 16 pieces

Ingredients

½ Cup fresh cilantro, chopped

1 cup sprouts (clover, alfalfa)

1 garlic clove, pressed

2 tablespoons ground brazil nuts or almonds

2 tablespoons flaked coconut

1 tablespoon coconut oil

Pinch cayenne pepper

Pinch sea salt

Pinch freshly ground black pepper

Zest and juice of 1 lemon

2 tablespoons ground flaxseed

1 to 2 tablespoons water

2 whole-wheat wraps, or corn wraps

Directions:

Put everything but the wraps in a food processor and pulse to combine. Or combine the **Ingredients** in a large bowl. Add the water, if needed, to help the mix come together.

Spread the mixture out over each wrap, roll it up, and place it in the fridge for 30 minutes to set.

Remove the rolls from the fridge and slice each into 8 pieces to serve as appetizers or sides with a soup or stew.

Get the best flavor by buying whole raw brazil nuts or almonds, toasting them lightly in a dry skillet or toaster oven, and then grinding them in a coffee grinder.

Nutrition (1 piece) calories: 66; total fat: 4g; carbs: 6g; fiber: 1g; protein: 2g

54. Tamari Almonds

Preparation time: 5 minutes
Cooking time: 15 minutes
Servings: 8

Ingredients

1 pound raw almonds

3 tablespoons tamari or soy sauce

2 tablespoons extra-virgin olive oil

1 tablespoon Nutritional yeast

1 to 2 teaspoons chili powder, to taste

Directions:

Preheat the oven to 400ºf.

Line a baking sheet with parchment paper.

In a medium bowl, combine the almonds, tamari, and olive oil until well coated.

Spread the almonds on the prepared baking sheet and roast for 10 to 15 minutes, until browned.

Cool for 10 minutes, then season with the Nutritional yeast and chili powder.

Transfer to a glass jar and close tightly with a lid.

Nutrition: calories: 364; fat: 32g; protein: 13g; carbohydrates: 13g; fiber: 7g; sugar: 3g; sodium: 381mg

55. Tempeh Taco Bites

Preparation time: 5 minutes
Cooking time: 45 minutes
Servings: 3 dozen

Ingredients

8 ounces tempeh

3 tablespoons soy sauce

2 teaspoons ground cumin

1 teaspoon chili powder

1 teaspoon dried oregano

1 tablespoon olive oil

1/2 cup finely minced onion

2 garlic cloves, minced

Salt and freshly ground black pepper

2 tablespoons tomato paste

1 chipotle chile in adobo, finely minced

1/4 cup hot water or vegetable broth, homemade or store-bought, plus more if needed

36 phyllo pastry cups, thawed

1/2 cup basic guacamole, homemade or store-bought

18 ripe cherry tomatoes, halved

Directions

In a medium saucepan of simmering water, cook the tempeh for 30 minutes. Drain well, then finely mince and place it in a bowl. Add the soy sauce, cumin, chili powder, and oregano. Mix well and set aside.

In a medium skillet, heat the oil over medium heat. Add the onion, cover, and cook for 5 minutes. Stir in the garlic, then add the tempeh mixture and cook, stirring, for 2 to 3 minutes. Season with salt and pepper to taste. Set aside.

In a small bowl, combine the tomato paste, chipotle, and the hot water or broth. Return tempeh mixture to heat and in stir tomato-chile mixture and cook for 10 to 15 minutes, stirring occasionally, until the liquid is absorbed.

The mixture should be fairly dry, but if it begins to stick to the pan, add a little more hot water, 1 tablespoon at a time. Taste, adjusting seasonings if necessary. Remove from the heat.

To assemble, fill the phyllo cups to the top with the tempeh filling, using about 2 teaspoons of filling in each. Top with a dollop of guacamole and a cherry tomato half and serve.

56. Mushroom Croustades

Preparation time: 10 minutes
Cooking time: 10 minutes
Servings: 12 croustades

Ingredients

12 thin slices whole-grain bread

1 tablespoon olive oil, plus more for brushing bread

2 medium shallots, chopped

2 garlic cloves, minced

12 ounces white mushrooms, chopped

1/4 cup chopped fresh parsley

1 teaspoon dried thyme

1 tablespoon soy sauce

Directions

Preheat the oven to 400°f. Using a 3-inch round pastry cutter or a drinking glass, cut a circle from each bread slice. Brush the bread circles with oil and press them firmly but gently into a mini-muffin tin. Bake until the bread is toasted, about 10 minutes.

Meanwhile, in a large skillet, heat the 1 tablespoon oil over medium heat. Add the shallots, garlic, and mushrooms and sauté for 5 minutes to soften the vegetables. Stir in the parsley, thyme, and soy sauce and cook until the liquid is absorbed, about 5 minutes longer. Spoon the mushroom mixture into the croustade cups and return to the oven for 3 to 5 minutes to heat through. Serve warm.

57. Stuffed Cherry Tomatoes

Preparation time: 15 minutes
Cooking time: 0 minutes
Servings: 6

Ingredients

2 pints cherry tomatoes, tops removed and centers scooped out

2 avocados, mashed

Juice of 1 lemon

½ Red bell pepper, minced

4 green onions (white and green parts), finely minced

1 tablespoon minced fresh tarragon

Pinch of sea salt

Directions:

Place the cherry tomatoes open-side up on a platter.

In a small bowl, -combine the avocado, lemon juice, bell pepper, scallions, tarragon, and salt.

Stir until well -combined. Scoop into the cherry tomatoes and serve immediately.

58. Spicy Black Bean Dip

Preparation time: 10 minutes
Cooking time: 0 minutes
Servings: 2 cups

Ingredients

1 (14-ounce) can black beans, drained and rinsed, or 1½ cups cooked

Zest and juice of 1 lime

1 tablespoon tamari, or soy sauce

¼ Cup water

¼ Cup fresh cilantro, chopped

1 teaspoon ground cumin

Pinch cayenne pepper

Directions:

Put the beans in a food processor (best choice) or blender, along with the lime zest and juice, tamari, and about ¼ cup of water.

Blend until smooth, then blend in the cilantro, cumin, and cayenne.

If you don't have a blender or prefer a different consistency, simply transfer it to a bowl once the beans have been puréed and stir in the spices, instead of forcing the blender.

Nutrition (1 cup) calories: 190; total fat: 1g; carbs: 35g; fiber: 12g; protein: 13g

59. French Onion Pastry Puffs

Preparation time: 10 minutes
Cooking time: 35 minutes - makes 24 puffs

Ingredients

2 tablespoons olive oil

2 medium sweet yellow onions, thinly sliced

1 garlic clove, minced

1 teaspoon chopped fresh rosemary

Salt and freshly ground black pepper

1 tablespoon capers

1 sheet frozen vegan puff pastry, thawed

18 pitted black olives, quartered

Directions

In a medium skillet, heat the oil over medium heat. Add the onions and garlic, season with rosemary and salt and pepper to taste. Cover and cook until very soft, stirring occasionally, about 20 minutes. Stir in the capers and set aside.

Preheat the oven to 400°f. Roll out the puff pastry and cut into 2- to 3-inch circles using a lightly floured pastry cutter or drinking glass. You should get about 2 dozen circles.

Arrange the pastry circles on baking sheets and top each with a heaping teaspoon of onion mixture, patting down to smooth the top.

Top with 3 olive quarters, arranged decoratively—either like flower petals emanating from the center or parallel to each other like 3 bars.

Bake until pastry is puffed and golden brown, about 15 minutes. Serve hot.

60. Cheezy Cashew–Roasted Red Pepper Toasts

Preparation time: 15 minutes
Cooking time: 0 minutes
Servings: 16 to 24 toasts

Ingredients

2 jarred roasted red peppers

1 cup unsalted cashews

1/4 cup water

1 tablespoon soy sauce

2 tablespoons chopped green onions

1/4 cup Nutritional yeast

2 tablespoons balsamic vinegar

2 tablespoons olive oil

Directions

Use canapé or cookie cutters to cut the bread into desired shapes about 2 inches wide. If you don't have a cutter, use a knife to cut the bread into squares, triangles, or rectangles. You should get 2 to 4 pieces out of each slice of bread. Toast the bread and set aside to cool.

Coarsely chop 1 red pepper and set aside. Cut the remaining pepper into thin strips or decorative shapes and set aside for garnish.

In a blender or food processor, grind the cashews to a fine powder. Add the water and soy sauce and process until smooth. Add the chopped red pepper and puree. Add the green onions, Nutritional yeast, vinegar, and oil and process until smooth and well blended.

Spread a spoonful of the pepper mixture onto each of the toasted bread pieces and top decoratively with the reserved pepper strips. Arrange on a platter or tray and serve.

61. Baked Potato Chips

Preparation time: 10 minutes
Cooking time: 30 minutes
Servings: 4

Ingredients

1 large russet potato
1 teaspoon paprika
½ Teaspoon garlic salt
¼ Teaspoon vegan sugar
¼ Teaspoon onion powder
¼ Teaspoon chipotle powder or chili powder
⅛ Teaspoon salt
⅛ Teaspoon ground mustard
⅛ Teaspoon ground cayenne pepper
1 teaspoon canola oil
⅛ Teaspoon liquid smoke

Directions:

Wash and peel the potato. Cut into thin, 1/10-inch slices (a mandoline slicer or the slicer blade in a food processor is helpful for consistently sized slices).

Fill a large bowl with enough very cold water to cover the potato. Transfer the potato slices to the bowl and soak for 20 minutes.

Preheat the oven to 400°f. Line a baking sheet with parchment paper.

In a small bowl, combine the paprika, garlic salt, sugar, onion powder, chipotle powder, salt, mustard, and cayenne.

Drain and rinse the potato slices and pat dry with a paper towel.

Transfer to a large bowl.

Add the canola oil, liquid smoke, and spice mixture to the bowl. Toss to coat.

Transfer the potatoes to the prepared baking sheet.

Bake for 15 minutes. Flip the chips over and bake for 15 minutes longer, until browned. Transfer the chips to 4 storage containers or large glass jars.

Let cool before closing the lids tightly.

Nutrition: calories: 89; fat: 1g; protein: 2g; carbohydrates: 18g; fiber: 2g; sugar: 1g; sodium: 65mg

62. Mushrooms Stuffed With Spinach And Walnuts

Preparation time: 10 minutes
Cooking time: 6 minutes
Servings: 4 to 6 servings

Ingredients

2 tablespoons olive oil

8 ounces white mushroom, lightly rinsed, patted dry, and stems reserved

1 garlic clove, minced

1 cup cooked spinach

1 cup finely chopped walnuts

1/2 cup unseasoned dry bread crumbs

Salt and freshly ground black pepper

Directions

Preheat the oven to 400°f. Lightly oil a large baking pan and set aside. In a large skillet, heat the oil over medium heat. Add the mushroom caps and cook for 2 minutes to soften slightly. Remove from the skillet and set aside.

Chop the mushroom stems and add to the same skillet. Add the garlic and cook over medium heat until softened, about 2 minutes. Stir in the spinach, walnuts, bread crumbs, and salt and pepper to taste. Cook for 2 minutes, stirring well to combine.

Fill the reserved mushroom caps with the stuffing mixture and arrange in the baking pan. Bake until the mushrooms are tender and the filling is hot, about 10 minutes. Serve hot.

63. Salsa Fresca

Preparation time: 15 minutes
Cooking time: 0 minutes
Servings: 4

Ingredients

3 large heirloom tomatoes or other fresh tomatoes, chopped
½ Red onion, finely chopped
½ Bunch cilantro, chopped
2 garlic cloves, minced
1 jalapeño, minced
Juice of 1 lime, or 1 tablespoon prepared lime juice
¼ Cup olive oil
Sea salt
Whole-grain tortilla chips, for serving

Directions:

In a small bowl, combine the tomatoes, onion, cilantro, garlic, jalapeño, lime juice, and olive oil and mix well. Allow to sit at room temperature for 15 minutes. Season with salt.

Serve with tortilla chips.

The salsa can be stored in an airtight container in the refrigerator for up to 1 week.

64. Guacamole

Preparation time: 10 minutes
Cooking time: 0 minutes
Servings: 2

Ingredients

2 ripe avocados

2 garlic cloves, pressed

Zest and juice of 1 lime

1 teaspoon ground cumin

Pinch sea salt

Pinch freshly ground black pepper

Pinch cayenne pepper (optional)

Directions:

Mash the avocados in a large bowl. Add the rest of the Ingredients and stir to combine.

Try adding diced tomatoes (cherry are divine), chopped scallions or chives, chopped fresh cilantro or basil, lemon rather than lime, paprika, or whatever you think would taste good!

Nutrition (1 cup) calories: 258; total fat: 22g; carbs: 18g; fiber: 11g; protein: 4g

65. Veggie Hummus Pinwheels

Preparation time: 10 minutes
Cooking time: 0 minutes
Servings: 3
Ingredients

3 whole-grain, spinach, flour, or gluten-free tortillas
3 large swiss chard leaves
¾ Cup edamame hummus or prepared hummus
¾ Cup shredded carrots

Directions:

Lay 1 tortilla flat on a cutting board.

Place 1 swiss chard leaf over the tortilla. Spread ¼ cup of hummus over the swiss chard. Spread ¼ cup of carrots over the hummus. Starting at one end of the tortilla, roll tightly toward the opposite side.

Slice each roll up into 6 pieces. Place in a single-serving storage container.

Repeat with the remaining tortillas and filling and seal the lids.

Nutrition: calories: 254; fat: 8g; protein: 10g; carbohydrates: 39g; fiber: 8g; sugar: 4g; sodium: 488mg

66. Asian Lettuce Rolls

Preparation time: 15 minutes
Cooking time: 5 minutes
Servings: 4

Ingredients

2 ounces rice noodles
2 tablespoons chopped thai basil
2 tablespoons chopped cilantro
1 garlic clove, minced
1 tablespoon minced fresh ginger
Juice of ½ lime, or 2 teaspoons prepared lime juice
2 tablespoons soy sauce
1 cucumber, julienned
2 carrots, peeled and julienned
8 leaves butter lettuce

Directions:

Cook the rice noodles according to package Directions.

In a small bowl, whisk together the basil, cilantro, garlic, ginger, lime juice, and soy sauce. Toss with the cooked noodles, cucumber, and carrots.

Divide the mixture evenly among lettuce leaves and roll.

Secure with a toothpick and serve immediately.

67. Pinto-Pecan Fireballs

Preparation time: 5 minutes
Cooking time: 30 minutes
Servings: about 20 pieces

Ingredients

1-1/2 cups cooked or 1 (15.5-ounce) can pinto beans, drained and rinsed

1/2 cup chopped pecans

1/4 cup minced green onions

1 garlic clove, minced

3 tablespoons wheat gluten flour (vital wheat gluten)

3 tablespoons unseasoned dry bread crumbs

4 tablespoons tabasco or other hot sauce

1/4 teaspoon salt

1/8 teaspoon ground cayenne

1/4 cup vegan margarine

Directions

Preheat the oven to 350°f. Lightly oil a 9 x 13-inch baking pan and set aside. Blot the drained beans well with a paper towel, pressing out any excess liquid. In a food processor, combine the pinto beans, pecans, green onions, garlic, flour, bread crumbs, 2 tablespoons of the tabasco, salt, and cayenne. Pulse until well combined, leaving some texture. Use your hands to roll the mixture firmly into 1-inch balls.

Place the balls in the prepared baking pan and bake until nicely browned, about 25 to 30 minutes, turning halfway through.

Meanwhile, in small saucepan, combine the remaining 2 tablespoons tabasco and the margarine and melt over low heat. Pour the sauce over the fireballs and bake 10 minutes longer. Serve immediately.

68. Sweet Potato Biscuits

Preparation time: 60 minutes
Cooking time: 10 minutes
Servings: 12 biscuits

Ingredients

1 medium sweet potato
3 tablespoons melted coconut oil, divided
1 tablespoon maple syrup
1 cup whole-wheat flour
2 teaspoons baking powder
Pinch sea salt

Directions:

Bake the sweet potato at 350°F for about 45 minutes, until tender.

Allow it to cool, then remove the flesh and mash.

Turn the oven up to 375°F and line a baking sheet with parchment paper or lightly grease it. Measure out 1 cup potato flesh.

In a medium bowl, combine the mashed sweet potato with 1½ tablespoons of the coconut oil and the maple syrup. Mix together the flour and baking powder in a separate medium bowl, then add the flour mixture to the potato mixture and blend well with a fork.

On a floured board, pat the mixture out into a ½-inch-thick circle and cut out 1-inch rounds, or simply drop spoonfuls of dough and pat them into rounds.

Put the rounds onto the prepared baking sheet. Brush the top of each with some of the remaining 1½ tablespoons melted coconut oil. Bake 10 minutes, or until lightly golden on top. Serve hot.

Nutrition (1 biscuit) calories: 116; total fat: 4g; carbs: 19g; fiber: 3g; protein: 3g

69. Lemon And Garlic Marinated Mushrooms

Preparation time: 15 minutes
Cooking time: 0 minutes
Servings: 4 servings

Ingredients

3 tablespoons olive oil

2 tablespoons fresh lemon juice

2 garlic cloves, crushed

1 teaspoon dried marjoram

1/2 teaspoon coarsely ground fennel seed

1/2 teaspoon salt

1/4 teaspoon freshly ground black pepper

8 ounces small white mushrooms, lightly rinsed, patted dry, and stemmed

1 tablespoon minced fresh parsley

Directions

In a medium bowl, whisk together the oil, lemon juice, garlic, marjoram, fennel seed, salt, and pepper. Add the mushrooms and parsley and stir gently until coated.

Cover and refrigerate for at least 2 hours or overnight. Stir well before serving.

70. Garlic Toast

Preparation time: 5 minutes
Cooking time: 5 minutes
Servings: 1 slice

Ingredients

1 teaspoon coconut oil, or olive oil

Pinch sea salt

1 to 2 teaspoons Nutritional yeast

1 small garlic clove, pressed, or ¼ teaspoon garlic powder

1 slice whole-grain bread

Directions:

In a small bowl, mix together the oil, salt, Nutritional yeast, and garlic.

You can either toast the bread and then spread it with the seasoned oil, or brush the oil on the bread and put it in a toaster oven to bake for 5 minutes.

If you're using fresh garlic, it's best to spread it onto the bread and then bake it.

Nutrition (1 slice) calories: 138; total fat: 6g; carbs: 16g; fiber: 4g; protein: 7g

71. Vietnamese-Style Lettuce Rolls

Preparation time: 15 minutes
Cooking time: 0 minutes
Servings: 4 servings

Ingredients

2 green onions

2 tablespoons soy sauce

2 tablespoons rice vinegar

1 teaspoon sugar

1/8 teaspoon crushed red pepper

3 tablespoons water

3 ounces rice vermicelli

4 to 6 soft green leaf lettuce leaves

1 medium carrot, shredded

1/2 medium english cucumber, peeled, seeded, and cut lengthwise into 1/4-inch strips

1/2 medium red bell pepper, cut into 1/4-inch strips

1 cup loosely packed fresh cilantro or basil leaves

Directions

Cut the green part off the green onions and cut them lengthwise into thin slices and set aside. Mince the white part of the green onions and transfer to a small bowl. Add the soy sauce, rice vinegar, sugar, crushed red pepper, and water. Stir to blend and set aside.

Soak the vermicelli in medium bowl of hot water until softened, about 1 minute. Drain the noodles well and cut them into 3-inch lengths. Set aside.

Place a lettuce leaf on a work surface and arrange a row of noodles in the center of the leaf, followed by a few strips of scallion greens, carrot, cucumber, bell pepper, and cilantro. Bring the bottom edge of the leaf over the filling and fold in the two short sides. Roll up gently but tightly. Place the roll seam side down on a serving platter. Repeat with

Remaining Ingredients. Serve with the dipping sauce.

72. Apple Crumble

Preparation time: 20 minutes
Cooking time: 25 minutes
Servings: 6
Ingredients

FOR THE FILLING

4 to 5 apples, cored and chopped (about 6 cups)

½ Cup unsweetened applesauce, or ¼ cup water

2 to 3 tablespoons unrefined sugar (coconut, date, sucanat, maple syrup)

1 teaspoon ground cinnamon

Pinch sea salt

FOR THE CRUMBLE

2 tablespoons almond butter, or cashew or sunflower seed butter

2 tablespoons maple syrup

1½ cups rolled oats

½ Cup walnuts, finely chopped

½ Teaspoon ground cinnamon

2 to 3 tablespoons unrefined granular sugar (coconut, date, sucanat)

Directions:

Preheat the oven to 350°f. Put the apples and applesauce in an 8-inch-square baking dish, and sprinkle with the sugar, cinnamon, and salt. Toss to combine.

In a medium bowl, mix together the nut butter and maple syrup until smooth and creamy. Add the oats, walnuts, cinnamon, and sugar and stir to coat, using your hands if necessary. (if you have a small food processor, pulse the oats and walnuts together before adding them to the mix.)

Sprinkle the topping over the apples, and put the dish in the oven.

Bake for 20 to 25 minutes, or until the fruit is soft and the topping is lightly browned.

Nutrition calories: 356; total fat: 17g; carbs: 49g; fiber: 7g; protein: 7g

73. Cashew-Chocolate Truffles

Preparation time: 15 minutes
Cooking time: 0 minutes • plus 1 hour to set
Servings: 12 truffles

Ingredients

1 cup raw cashews, soaked in water overnight
¾ Cup pitted dates
2 tablespoons coconut oil
1 cup unsweetened shredded coconut, divided
1 to 2 tablespoons cocoa powder, to taste

Directions:

In a food processor, combine the cashews, dates, coconut oil, ½ cup of shredded coconut, and cocoa powder. Pulse until fully incorporated; it will resemble chunky cookie dough. Spread the remaining ½ cup of shredded coconut on a plate.

Form the mixture into tablespoon-size balls and roll on the plate to cover with the shredded coconut. Transfer to a parchment paper–lined plate or baking sheet. Repeat to make 12 truffles.

Place the truffles in the refrigerator for 1 hour to set. Transfer the truffles to a storage container or freezer-safe bag and seal.

Nutrition (1 truffle): calories 238: fat: 18g; protein: 3g; carbohydrates: 16g; fiber: 4g; sugar: 9g; sodium: 9mg

74. Banana Chocolate Cupcakes

Preparation time: 20 minutes
Cooking time: 20 minutes
Servings: 12 cupcakes

Ingredients

3 medium bananas

1 cup non-dairy milk

2 tablespoons almond butter

1 teaspoon apple cider vinegar

1 teaspoon pure vanilla extract

1¼ cups whole-grain flour

½ Cup rolled oats

¼ Cup coconut sugar (optional)

1 teaspoon baking powder

½ Teaspoon baking soda

½ Cup unsweetened cocoa powder

¼ Cup chia seeds, or sesame seeds

Pinch sea salt

¼ Cup dark chocolate chips, dried cranberries, or raisins (optional)

Directions:

Preheat the oven to 350°f. Lightly grease the cups of two 6-cup muffin tins or line with paper muffin cups.

Put the bananas, milk, almond butter, vinegar, and vanilla in a blender and purée until smooth. Or stir together in a large bowl until smooth and creamy.

Put the flour, oats, sugar (if using), baking powder, baking soda, cocoa powder, chia seeds, salt, and chocolate chips in another large bowl, and stir to combine. Mix together the wet and dry Ingredients, stirring as little as possible. Spoon into muffin cups, and bake for 20 to 25 minutes. Take the cupcakes out of the oven and let them cool fully before taking out of the muffin tins, since they'll be very moist.

Nutrition (1 cupcake) calories: 215; total fat: 6g; carbs: 39g; fiber: 9g; protein: 6g

75. Minty Fruit Salad

Preparation time: 15 minutes
Cooking time: 5 minutes
Servings: 4
Ingredients

¼ Cup lemon juice (about 2 small lemons)

4 teaspoons maple syrup or agave syrup

2 cups chopped pineapple

2 cups chopped strawberries

2 cups raspberries

1 cup blueberries

8 fresh mint leaves

Directions:

Beginning with 1 mason jar, add the Ingredients in this order:

1 tablespoon of lemon juice, 1 teaspoon of maple syrup, ½ cup of pineapple, ½ cup of strawberries, ½ cup of raspberries, ¼ cup of blueberries, and 2 mint leaves.

Repeat to fill 3 more jars. Close the jars tightly with lids.

Place the airtight jars in the refrigerator for up to 3 days.

Nutrition: calories: 138; fat: 1g; protein: 2g; carbohydrates: 34g; fiber: 8g; sugar: 22g; sodium: 6mg

76. Mango Coconut Cream Pie

Preparation time: 20 minutes • chill time: 30 minutes
Servings: 8
Ingredients
FOR THE CRUST

½ Cup rolled oats

1 cup cashews

1 cup soft pitted dates

FOR THE FILLING

1 cup canned coconut milk

½ Cup water

2 large mangos, peeled and chopped, or about 2 cups frozen chunks

½ Cup unsweetened shredded coconut

Directions:

Put all the crust Ingredients in a food processor and pulse until it holds together. If you don't have a food processor, chop everything as finely as possible and use ½ cup cashew or almond butter in place of half the cashews. Press the mixture down firmly into an 8-inch pie or springform pan.

Put the all filling Ingredients in a blender and purée until smooth (about 1 minute). It should be very thick, so you may have to stop and stir until it's smooth.

Pour the filling into the crust, use a rubber spatula to smooth the top, and put the pie in the freezer until set, about 30 minutes. Once frozen, it should be set out for about 15 minutes to soften before serving.

Top with a batch of coconut whipped cream scooped on top of the pie once it's set. Finish it off with a sprinkling of toasted shredded coconut.

Nutrition (1 slice) calories: 427; total fat: 28g; carbs: 45g; fiber: 6g; protein: 8g

77. Cherry-Vanilla Rice Pudding (pressure cooker)

Preparation time: 5 minutes

Serves 4-6

Ingredients

1 cup short-grain brown rice

1¾ cups nondairy milk, plus more as needed

1½ cups water

4 tablespoons unrefined sugar or pure maple syrup (use 2 tablespoons if you use a sweetened milk), plus more as needed

1 teaspoon vanilla extract (use ½ teaspoon if you use vanilla milk)

Pinch salt

¼ Cup dried cherries *or* ½ cup fresh or frozen pitted cherries

Directions

In your electric pressure cooker's cooking pot, combine the rice, milk, water, sugar, vanilla, and salt.

High pressure for 30 minutes. Close and lock the lid, and select high pressure for 30 minutes.

Pressure release. Once the cook time is complete, let the pressure release naturally, about 20 minutes. Unlock and remove the lid. Stir in the cherries and put the lid back on loosely for about 10 minutes. Serve, adding more milk or sugar, as desired.

Nutrition calories: 177; total fat: 1g; protein: 3g; sodium: 27mg; fiber: 2g

78. Mint Chocolate Chip Sorbet

Preparation time: 5 minutes
Cooking time: 0 minutes
Servings: 1

Ingredients

1 frozen banana

1 tablespoon almond butter, or peanut butter, or other nut or seed butter

2 tablespoons fresh mint, minced

¼ Cup or less non-dairy milk (only if needed)

2 to 3 tablespoons non-dairy chocolate chips, or cocoa nibs

2 to 3 tablespoons goji berries (optional)

Directions:

Put the banana, almond butter, and mint in a food processor or blender and purée until smooth.

Add the non-dairy milk if needed to keep blending (but only if needed, as this will make the texture less solid). Pulse the chocolate chips and goji berries (if using) into the mix so they're roughly chopped up.

Nutrition calories: 212; total fat: 10g; carbs: 31g; fiber: 4g; protein: 3g

79. Peach-Mango Crumble (pressure cooker)

Preparation time: 10 minutes

Serves 4-6

Ingredients

3 cups chopped fresh or frozen peaches

3 cups chopped fresh or frozen mangos

4 tablespoons unrefined sugar or pure maple syrup, divided

1 cup gluten-free rolled oats

½ Cup shredded coconut, sweetened or unsweetened

2 tablespoons coconut oil or vegan margarine

Directions

In a 6- to 7-inch round baking dish, toss together the peaches, mangos, and 2 tablespoons of sugar. In a food processor, combine the oats, coconut, coconut oil, and remaining 2 tablespoons of sugar. Pulse until combined. (if you use maple syrup, you'll need less coconut oil. Start with just the syrup and add oil if the mixture isn't sticking together.) Sprinkle the oat mixture over the fruit mixture.

Cover the dish with aluminum foil. Put a trivet in the bottom of your electric pressure cooker's cooking pot and pour in a cup or two of water. Using a foil sling or silicone helper handles, lower the pan onto the trivet.

High pressure for 6 minutes. Close and lock the lid, and select high pressure for 6 minutes.

Pressure release. Once the cook time is complete, quick release the pressure. Unlock and remove the lid.

Let cool for a few minutes before carefully lifting out the dish with oven mitts or tongs. Scoop out portions to serve.

Nutrition calories: 321; total fat: 18g; protein: 4g; sodium: 2mg; fiber: 7g

80. Zesty Orange-Cranberry Energy Bites

Preparation time: 10 minutes • chill time: 15 minutes
Servings: 12 bites

Ingredients

2 tablespoons almond butter, or cashew or sunflower seed butter

2 tablespoons maple syrup, or brown rice syrup

¾ Cup cooked quinoa

¼ Cup sesame seeds, toasted

1 tablespoon chia seeds

½ Teaspoon almond extract, or vanilla extract

Zest of 1 orange

1 tablespoon dried cranberries

¼ Cup ground almonds

Directions:

In a medium bowl, mix together the nut or seed butter and syrup until smooth and creamy. Stir in the rest of the Ingredients, and mix to make sure the consistency is holding together in a ball. Form the mix into 12 balls.

Place them on a baking sheet lined with parchment or waxed paper and put in the fridge to set for about 15 minutes.

If your balls aren't holding together, it's likely because of the moisture content of your cooked quinoa. Add more nut or seed butter mixed with syrup until it all sticks together.

Nutrition (1 bite) calories: 109; total fat: 7g; carbs: 11g; fiber: 3g; protein: 3g

81. Almond-Date Energy Bites

Preparation time: 5 minutes • chill time: 15 minutes
Servings: 24 bites

Ingredients

1 cup dates, pitted
1 cup unsweetened shredded coconut
¼ Cup chia seeds
¾ Cup ground almonds
¼ Cup cocoa nibs, or non-dairy chocolate chips

Directions:

Purée everything in a food processor until crumbly and sticking together, pushing down the sides whenever necessary to keep it blending. If you don't have a food processor, you can mash soft medjool dates. But if you're using harder baking dates, you'll have to soak them and then try to purée them in a blender.

Form the mix into 24 balls and place them on a baking sheet lined with parchment or waxed paper. Put in the fridge to set for about 15 minutes. Use the softest dates you can find. Medjool dates are the best for this purpose. The hard dates you see in the baking aisle of your supermarket are going to take a long time to blend up. If you use those, try soaking them in water for at least an hour before you start, and then draining.

Nutrition (1 bite) calories: 152; total fat: 11g; carbs: 13g; fiber: 5g; protein: 3g

Pumpkin pie cups (pressure cooker)

Preparation time: 5 minutes

Serves 4-6

Ingredients

1 cup canned pumpkin purée

1 cup nondairy milk

6 tablespoons unrefined sugar or pure maple syrup (less if using sweetened milk), plus more for sprinkling

¼ Cup spelt flour or all-purpose flour

½ Teaspoon pumpkin pie spice

Pinch salt

Directions

In a medium bowl, stir together the pumpkin, milk, sugar, flour, pumpkin pie spice, and salt. Pour the mixture into 4 heat-proof ramekins. Sprinkle a bit more sugar on the top of each, if you like. Put a trivet in the bottom of your electric pressure cooker's cooking pot and pour in a cup or two of water. Place the ramekins onto the trivet, stacking them if needed (3 on the bottom, 1 on top).

High pressure for 6 minutes. Close and lock the lid, and select high pressure for 6 minutes.

Pressure release. Once the cook time is complete, quick release the pressure. Unlock and remove the lid. Let cool for a few minutes before carefully lifting out the ramekins with oven mitts or tongs. Let cool for at least 10 minutes before serving.

Nutrition calories: 129; total fat: 1g; protein: 3g; sodium: 39mg; fiber: 3g

Coconut and almond truffles

Preparation time: 15 minutes
Cooking time: 0 minutes
Servings: 8 truffles

Ingredients

1 cup pitted dates

1 cup almonds

½ Cup sweetened cocoa powder, plus extra for coating

½ Cup unsweetened shredded coconut

¼ Cup pure maple syrup

1 teaspoon vanilla extract

1 teaspoon almond extract

¼ Teaspoon sea salt

Directions:

In the bowl of a food processor, combine all the **Ingredients** and process until smooth. Chill the mixture for about 1 hour.

Roll the mixture into balls and then roll the balls in cocoa powder to coat.

Serve immediately or keep chilled until ready to serve.

Fudgy Brownies (Pressure cooker)

Preparation time: 10 minutes

Serves 4-6

Ingredients

3 ounces dairy-free dark chocolate

1 tablespoon coconut oil or vegan margarine

½ Cup applesauce

2 tablespoons unrefined sugar

⅓ Cup all-purpose flour

½ Teaspoon baking powder

Pinch salt

Directions

Put a trivet in your electric pressure cooker's cooking pot and pour in a cup or two of two of water. Select sauté or simmer. In a large heat-proof glass or ceramic bowl, combine the chocolate and coconut oil. Place the bowl over the top of your pressure cooker, as you would a double boiler. Stir occasionally until the chocolate is melted, then turn off the pressure cooker. Stir the applesauce and sugar into the chocolate mixture. Add the flour, baking powder, and salt and stir just until combined. Pour the batter into 3 heat-proof ramekins. Put them in a heat-proof dish and cover with aluminum foil. Using a foil sling or silicone helper handles, lower the dish onto the trivet. (alternately, cover each ramekin with foil and place them directly on the trivet, without the dish.)

High pressure for 6 minutes. Close and lock the lid, and select high pressure for 5 minutes.

Pressure release. Once the cook time is complete, quick release the pressure. Unlock and remove the lid.

Let cool for a few minutes before carefully lifting out the dish, or ramekins, with oven mitts or tongs. Let cool for a few minutes more before serving.

Top with fresh raspberries and an extra drizzle of melted chocolate.

Nutrition calories: 316; total fat: 14g; protein: 5g; sodium: 68mg; fiber: 5g

Chocolate macaroons

Preparation time: 10 minutes
Cooking time: 15 minutes

Servings: 8 macaroons

Ingredients

1 cup unsweetened shredded coconut

2 tablespoons cocoa powder

⅔ Cup coconut milk

¼ Cup agave

Pinch of sea salt

Directions:

Preheat the oven to 350°f. Line a baking sheet with parchment paper. In a medium saucepan, cook all the Ingredients over -medium-high heat until a firm dough is formed. Scoop the dough into balls and place on the baking sheet.

Bake for 15 minutes, remove from the oven, and let cool on the baking sheet.

Serve cooled macaroons or store in a tightly sealed container for up to

82. Chocolate Pudding

Preparation time: 5 minutes
Cooking time: 0 minutes
Servings: 1

Ingredients

1 banana
2 to 4 tablespoons nondairy milk
2 tablespoons unsweetened cocoa powder
2 tablespoons sugar (optional)
½ Ripe avocado or 1 cup silken tofu (optional)

Directions:

In a small blender, combine the banana, milk, cocoa powder, sugar (if using), and avocado (if using). Purée until smooth. Alternatively, in a small bowl, mash the banana very well, and stir in the remaining Ingredients.

Nutrition calories: 244; protein: 4g; total fat: 3g; saturated fat: 1g; carbohydrates: 59g; fiber: 8g

Lime and watermelon granita

Preparation time: 15 minutes • chilling time: 6 hours •
Servings: 4

Ingredients

8 cups seedless -watermelon chunks
Juice of 2 limes, or 2 tablespoons prepared lime juice
½ Cup sugar
Strips of lime zest, for garnish

Directions:

In a blender or food processor, combine the watermelon, lime juice, and sugar and process until smooth. You may have to do this in two batches. After processing, stir well to combine both batches.

Pour the mixture into a 9-by-13-inch glass dish. Freeze for 2 to 3 hours. Remove from the freezer and use a fork to scrape the top layer of ice. Leave the shaved ice on top and return to the freezer.

In another hour, remove from the freezer and repeat. Do this a few more times until all the ice is scraped up. Serve frozen, garnished with strips of lime zest.

83. Coconut-Banana Pudding

Preparation time: 4 minutes
Cooking time: 5 minutes • overnight to set
Servings: 4

Ingredients

3 bananas, divided
1 (13.5-ounce) can full-fat coconut milk
¼ Cup organic cane sugar
1 tablespoon cornstarch
1 teaspoon vanilla extract
2 pinches sea salt
6 drops natural yellow food coloring (optional)
Ground cinnamon, for garnish

Directions:

Combine 1 banana, the coconut milk, sugar, cornstarch, vanilla, and salt in a blender. Blend until smooth and creamy. If you're using the food coloring, add it to the blender now and blend until the color is evenly dispersed.

Transfer to a saucepot and bring to a boil over medium-high heat. Immediately reduce to a simmer and whisk for 3 minutes, or until the mixture thickens to a thin pudding and sticks to a spoon.

Transfer the mixture to a container and allow to cool for 1 hour. Cover and refrigerate overnight to set. When you're ready to serve, slice the remaining 2 bananas and build individual servings as follows: pudding, banana slices, pudding, and so on until a single-serving dish is filled to the desired level. Sprinkle with ground cinnamon.

84. Spiced Apple Chia Pudding

Preparation time: 5 minutes • chill time: 30 minutes
Servings: 1
Ingredients

½ Cup unsweetened applesauce
¼ Cup nondairy milk or canned coconut milk
1 tablespoon chia seeds
1½ teaspoons sugar
Pinch ground cinnamon or pumpkin pie spice

Directions:

In a small bowl, stir together the applesauce, milk, chia seeds, sugar, and cinnamon. Enjoy as is, or let sit for 30 minutes so the chia seeds soften and expand.

Nutrition calories: 153; protein: 3g; total fat: 5g; saturated fat: 1g; carbohydrates: 26g; fiber: 10g

Caramelized pears with balsamic glaze

Preparation time: 5 minutes
Cooking time: 15 minutes

Servings: 4

Ingredients

1 cup balsamic vinegar
¼ Cup plus 3 tablespoons brown sugar
¼ Teaspoon grated nutmeg
Pinch of sea salt
¼ Cup coconut oil
4 pears, cored and cut into slices

Directions:

In a medium saucepan, heat the balsamic vinegar, ¼ cup of the brown sugar, the nutmeg, and salt over medium-high heat, stirring to thoroughly incorporate the sugar. Allow to simmer, stirring occasionally, until the glaze reduces by half, 10 to 15 minutes.

Meanwhile, heat the coconut oil in a large sauté pan over medium-high heat until it shimmers. Add the pears to the pan in a single layer. Cook until they turn golden, about 5 minutes. Add the remaining 3 tablespoons brown sugar and continue to cook, stirring occasionally, until the pears caramelize, about 5 minutes more.

Place the pears on a plate. Drizzle with balsamic glaze and serve.

85. Salted Coconut-Almond Fudge

Preparation time: 5 minutes • set time: 1 hour •
Servings: 12

Ingredients

¾ Cup creamy almond butter

½ Cup maple syrup

⅓ Cup coconut oil, softened or melted

6 tablespoons fair-trade unsweetened cocoa powder

1 teaspoon coarse or flaked sea salt

Directions:

Line a loaf pan with a double layer of plastic wrap. Place one layer horizontally in the pan with a generous amount of overhang, and the second layer vertically with a generous amount of overhang.

In a medium bowl, gently mix together the almond butter, maple syrup, and coconut oil until well combined and smooth. Add the cocoa powder and gently stir it into the mixture until well combined and creamy.

Pour the mixture into the prepared pan and sprinkle with the sea salt. Bring the overflowing edges of the plastic wrap over the top of the fudge to completely cover it. Place the pan in the freezer for at least 1 hour or overnight, until the fudge is firm.

Remove the pan from the freezer and lift the fudge out of the pan using the plastic-wrap overhangs to pull it out. Transfer to a cutting board and cut into 1-inch pieces.

86. Caramelized Bananas

Preparation time: 5 minutes
Cooking time: 10 minutes
Servings: 2

Ingredients

2 tablespoons vegan margarine or coconut oil

2 bananas, peeled, halved crosswise and then lengthwise

2 tablespoons dark brown sugar, demerara sugar, or coconut sugar

2 tablespoons spiced apple cider

Chopped walnuts, for topping

Directions:

Melt the margarine in a nonstick skillet over medium heat. Add the bananas, and cook for 2 minutes. Flip, and cook for 2 minutes more.

Sprinkle the sugar and cider into the oil around the bananas, and cook for 2 to 3 minutes, until the sauce thickens and caramelizes around the bananas. Carefully scoop the bananas into small bowls, and drizzle with any remaining liquid in the skillet. Sprinkle with walnuts.

Nutrition calories: 384; protein: 4g; total fat: 24g; saturated fat: 13g; carbohydrates: 46g; fiber: 5g

Mixed berries and cream

Preparation time: 10 minutes
Cooking time: 0 minutes
Servings: 4
Ingredients

Two 15-ounce cans full-fat coconut milk

3 tablespoons agave

½ Teaspoon vanilla extract

1 pint fresh blueberries

1 pint fresh raspberries

1 pint fresh strawberries, sliced

Directions:

Refrigerate the coconut milk overnight. When you open the can, the liquid will have separated from the solids. Spoon out the solids and reserve the liquid for another purpose.

In a medium bowl, whisk the agave and vanilla extract into the coconut solids. Divide the berries among four bowls. Top with the coconut cream. Serve immediately.

87. Peanut Butter Cups

Preparation time: 20 minutes
Cooking time: 0 minutes
Servings: 12 cups

Ingredients

1½ cups vegan chocolate chips, divided

½ Cup peanut butter, almond or cashew butter, or sunflower seed butter

¼ Cup packed brown sugar

2 tablespoons nondairy milk

Directions:

Line the cups of a muffin tin with paper liners or reusable silicone cups.

In a small microwave-safe bowl, heat ¾ cup of the chocolate chips on high power for 1 minute. Stir. Continue heating in 30-second increments, stirring after each, until the chocolate is melted.

Pour about 1½ teaspoons of melted chocolate into each prepared muffin cup. Set aside, and allow them to harden.

In a small bowl, stir together the peanut butter, brown sugar, and milk until smooth. Scoop about 1½ teaspoons of the mixture on top of the chocolate base in each cup. It's okay if the chocolate is not yet hardened.

Melt the remaining ¾ cup of chocolate chips using the **Directions** in step 1;pour another 1½ teaspoons of chocolate on top of the peanut butter in each cup, softly spreading it to cover. Let the cups sit until the chocolate hardens, about 15 minutes in the refrigerator or several hours on the counter. Leftovers will keep in the refrigerator for up to 2 weeks.

Nutrition (1 cup) calories: 227; protein: 4g; total fat: 14g; saturated fat: 6g; carbohydrates: 22g; fiber: 3g

Spiced rhubarb sauce

Preparation time: 10 minutes
Cooking time: 15 minutes
Servings: 4

Ingredients

½ Cup water

½ Cup sugar

¼ Teaspoon grated nutmeg

¼ Teaspoon ground ginger

¼ Teaspoon ground cinnamon

1 pound rhubarb, cut into ½- to 1-inch pieces

Directions

In a large saucepan, bring the water, sugar, nutmeg, ginger, and cinnamon to a boil. Add the rhubarb and cook over medium-high heat, stirring frequently, until the rhubarb is soft and saucy, about 10 minutes. Chill for at least 30 minutes before serving.

88. Chocolate-Coconut Bars

Preparation time: 20 minutes • chill time: 20 minutes
Servings: 16 bars

Ingredients

¼ Cup coconut oil or unsalted vegan margarine, plus more for preparing the baking dish (optional)

2 cups unsweetened shredded coconut

¼ Cup sugar

2 tablespoons maple syrup or *simple syrup*

1 cup vegan chocolate chips

Directions:

Coat the bottom and sides of an 8-9 inch-square baking-dish with coconut oil or line it with parchment paper, set aside.

In a bowl, stir the coconut, sugar, maple syrup, and coconut oil. Transfer the mixture to the prepared baking dish, and press it down firmly with the back of a spoon.

Heat the chocolate chips on high power for 1 minute, (in a microwave-safe bowl). Stir. Continue heating in 30-second increments, stir, until the chocolate is melted. Pour the melted chocolate over the coconut base, and let it sit until the chocolate hardens, about 20 minutes. Cut into 16 bars. Keep covered and refrigerated for up to 1 week.

Nutrition (1 bar) calories: 305; protein: 3g; total fat: 26g; saturated fat: 22g; carbohydrates: 19g; fiber: 6g

SAUCES AND DIPS
89. Cucumber Bites

Preparation time: 10 minutes (excluding soaking time)
Soaking time: 1-3 hours
Servings: 14 bites
Ingredients:

1 cup almonds – soaked 1-3 hours

¼ Cup cashew nuts – soaked 1-3 hours

Juice of 1 lemon

1 clove garlic –minced

Salt & pepper

1 tsp. Olive oil

1 large cucumber – sliced into approximately 1 inch pieces

1 tomato – diced

½ Cup fresh parsley – roughly chopped

Preparation:

Soak almonds and cashew nuts in warm water for 1-3 hours. The longer you soak them, the softer and creamier they will be.

Put all Ingredients (except cucumber, parsley and tomato) into a blender or food processor.

Blend or process until you get a creamy paste.

If the mix is too thick for your likings you can add a little bit of water.

Remove the mixture from the blender.

Add the diced tomato and fresh parsley and gently mix with a spoon.

Scoop one spoonful of mixture onto each cucumber slice.

8. Sprinkle with black pepper and serve.

90. Broccoli Crispy Bread

Preparation time: 5 minutes
Cooking time: 30 minutes
Servings: 3-4

Ingredients:

4 cups of broccoli florets – cut into chunks

3 tbsp. Nutritional yeast

1 tbsp. Extra virgin olive oil

2 tbsp. Chia seeds

1 tsp. Baking powder

Salt & pepper

½ Cup fresh basil

Preparation:

Preheat oven to 375f.

Soak the chia seeds with 6 tablespoons of water for about 5 minutes.

Put broccoli into a food processor and pulse until you get a texture similar to rice.

Add Nutritional yeast, basil, salt and pepper, and pulse until Ingredients are well combined.

Transfer the mix into a bowl, add olive oil, baking powder, chia seeds and stir well.

Line a baking tray with a sheet of baking paper.

Pour the dough onto the baking paper and spread evenly. The thinner you make it, the crispier it will be.

Bake in the oven for approximately 30 minute until golden and crispy. Make sure it is cooked in the middle.

Remove from the oven and cut into bars.

Enjoy while still warm or cold.

91. Roasted Pumpkin Seeds

Preparation time: 5 minutes
Cooking time: 25 minutes
Servings: as many as you'd like
Ingredients:
Pumpkin seeds
Extra virgin olive oil
Salt & pepper
Preparation:
Preheat oven to 350f.
Line a baking tray with baking paper or aluminium foil. Either will do.
 Place the seeds into a bowl, drizzle with not too much oil but enough to evenly coat them.
Sprinkle with salt and pepper and toss well together.
Pour the seeds onto the baking tray and roast in the oven for approximately 20 minutes or until they become very lightly brown. Keep an eye on them not to burn them.
During cooking remove the tray a few times to stir the seeds.
When completely roasted, remove from oven and let them cool.
Enjoy as nibbles or sprinkle on your salad or soup.

92. Multi Seeds Crackers

Preparation time: 10 minutes
Cooking time: 1 hour
Servings: 20-30 crackers (depending on your cuts)
Ingredients:
½ Cup chia seeds
½ Cup sunflower seeds
½ Cup pumpkin seeds
½ Cup sesame seeds
1 cup water
1 large clove garlic or 2 small – minced
Salt & pepper

Preparation:
Preheat oven to 300f.
Put all seeds into a large bowl and add water. Stir well until combined.
Let the seeds rest for 3-5 minutes until the chia seeds absorb the water.
Stir again. There should be no more water on the bottom of the bowl.
Use a spatula to spread the mixture onto the baking paper. Spread into two rectangles approximately 12"x 7" in size and approximately 1/8 to ¼ inch thick.
Sprinkle with salt and pepper.
Bake in the oven for 35 minutes.
Remove from oven and turn the rectangles around very carefully with a spatula.
Put back in the oven and back for another 25-35 minutes.
Keep an eye on them to make sure they don't burn.
Remove from oven when the edges are lightly golden.
Set aside to cool down for approximately 10 minutes.
Break the rectangles into crackers and let to cool completely.

You can store these crackers in an airtight container for up to 1 month, but we honestly think they will not last you that long as they are too moreish!

93. Almond Cauliflower

Preparation time: 5 minutes
Cooking time: 30 minutes
Servings: 4
Ingredients:
4 cups cauliflower florets – chopped into bite size chunks
1 tbsp. Extra virgin olive oil
2 tbsp. Almonds – chopped in very small pieces

Preparation:
Preheat oven to 425f.

Line a baking tray with baking paper.

Place cauliflower into a bowl, add olive oil, salt and pepper, almonds and toss everything well together.

Pour the cauliflower onto the baking paper.

Bake in oven for approximately 30 minutes or until golden brown and soft. Stir occasionally.

Remove from oven, sprinkle with ground black pepper and serve.

94. Tahini Dressing

Preparation time: 5 minutes
Servings: 4-5
Ingredients:
¼ Cup tahini paste
Juice of 1 lemon
1 tbsp. Apple cider vinegar
2 tbsp. Extra virgin olive oil
2 clove of garlic – minced
Salt & pepper

Preparation:
Place all Ingredients into a blender (except for water).
Blend until creamy.
If the dressing is too thick, add a little bit of water until it reaches the desired consistency.

95. Lemon & Mustard Vinaigrette

Preparation time: 5 minutes

Servings: 6 tablespoons

Ingredients:

Juice of 1 lemon

½ Tsp. Dijon mustard

4 tbsp. Extra virgin olive oil

Salt & pepper

Preparation:

Put lemon juice, mustard, salt and pepper into a bowl.

Whisk well until combined.

While whisking, drizzle in the extra virgin olive oil.

Keep whisking vigorously until all Ingredients are combined and you have a medium creamy dressing.

The dressing should be ready at this point. You can taste and adjust any of the Ingredients to taste.

96. Cheesy Sauce

Preparation time: 5 minutes
Servings: 4
Ingredients:
2 tbsp. Extra virgin olive oil
2 tbsp. Nutritional yeast
Juice of 1 lemon
Salt & pepper
Preparation:
Combine all Ingredients together into a bowl and whisk vigorously.

Serve as an accompaniment to your dishes.

97. Chimichurri Style Sauce

Preparation time: 1-2 minutes
Cooking time: 5 minutes
Servings: 2/3 cup
Ingredients:
½ Cup extra virgin olive oil

1 tsp. Fresh rosemary

1 tsp. Fresh oregano

2 medium cloves garlic – crushed

2 tsp. Smoked paprika

1 bay leaf

¼ Tsp. Sea salt

1 tbsp. Lemon juice

Pinch of black pepper flakes

Preparation:

Put the herbs into a mortar and pestle and lightly pound them. If you do not have a mortar and pestle you can chop them very finely.

Pour olive oil into a pan and warm over medium-low heat.

When oil is hot, remove from heat.

Stir paprika, black pepper flakes, bay leaf and a pinch of salt into the oil.

Add herbs and lemon juice.

Put the sauce into a jar in the fridge and leave it to infuse for a couple of days before using.

98. Peanut Sauce

Preparation time: 10 minutes
Cooking time: 5 minutes
Servings: 1 cup
Ingredients:
½ Cup creamy peanut butter
2 tbsp. Thai red curry paste
¾ Cup coconut milk
2tbsp. Apple cider vinegar
1/2 tbsp. Coconut palm sugar
2 tbsp. Ground peanuts
Salt

Preparation:
Add all Ingredients together into a saucepan and whisk well.

Transfer the pan to the stove and heat up the mix over a low heat while continuing whisking.

Keep a constant eye on the sauce and as soon as it starts bubbling remove from heat. If you like the sauce more liquid, add a little bit of water and whisk. Keep adding water bit by bit until it reaches your desired consistency.

Move the sauce into a bowl and top with ground peanuts.

99. Spicy Almond & Garlic Dip

Preparation time: 5 minutes

Soaking time: overnight

Servings: 1 large cup

Ingredients:

1 cup raw almonds

1 cup almond milk

2 cloves garlic

½ Tsp. Chili powder

¼ Tsp. Smoked paprika

Pinch of salt

Pinch of cayenne pepper

Preparation:

Soak almonds overnight.

Put all Ingredients into a blender.

Blend until smooth and creamy.

You can use immediately or refrigerate covered.

100. Cauliflower Hummus

Preparation time: 5 minutes
Cooking time: 5 minutes
Servings: 2 cups
Ingredients:
4 cups cauliflower stems and florets – chopped
2 tbsp. Tahini paste
5 tbsp. Extra virgin olive oil
Juice of 2 lemons
Salt & pepper
Pinch of cumin

Preparation:
Steam or lightly boil cauliflower for approximately 5 minutes or until soft.

Drain and let it cool down completely.

Combine cauliflower, tahini paste, extra virgin olive oil, lemon juice and cumin into a food processor. Process until creamy. Alternatively, you can use a blender.

Add salt and pepper to taste.

You might want to taste it and add more lemon juice or olive oil according to taste.

Serve with raw vegetables.

101. Eggplant & Walnut Spread

Preparation time: 10-15 minutes
Cooking time: 45 minutes
Servings: 1 large cup
Ingredients:
2 x medium round eggplants
1 tbsp. Extra virgin olive oil
1 cup walnuts – chopped
2 cloves garlic
Juice of 1 large lemon
Salt & pepper
1 tsp. Cumin
1/3 cup tahini paste
½ Cup fresh parsley leaves

Preparation:
Preheat oven to 375f.
Place eggplants on a baking tray and rub them with the olive oil.
Stab them with a knife a couple times.
Roast for 45 minutes until they look deflated and wrinkled.
In the meantime, toast the walnuts in a pan over medium-high heat for 3-4 minutes. Leave to cool.
When eggplant is cooked, remove from oven and let it cool down.
Cut the eggplants in half and scoop the flesh out into a food processor.
Add walnuts and all other Ingredients. Process until obtaining a paste.
Serve into a bowl with a drizzle of extra virgin olive oil accompanied by crackers or raw vegetables.

102. Coconut Yogurt Dip

Preparation time: 10 minutes
Servings: 2 cups
Ingredients:
1 ½ cup coconut yogurt
1 large cucumber – peeled and cut into chunks
3 cloves garlic
Juice of 1 lemon
2 tbsp. Extra virgin olive oil
½ Cup fresh coriander – finely chopped
Salt & pepper

Preparation:
Place all Ingredients (except coriander) into a blender and blend until smooth.

Add salt and pepper to taste and the coriander.

Mix well with a spoon.

Refrigerate for about 1 hour to let the flavors infuse.

Stir the dip well before serving.

103. Olive Tapenade

Preparation time: 5 minutes
Servings: 1 cup
Ingredients:

½ Cup black olives

½ Cup green olives

2 cloves garlic

1tsp. Lemon juice

Ground black pepper

Preparation:

Put all Ingredients together into a food processor and process for few seconds. You basically want all Ingredients finely chopped and well mixed together. Be careful not processes for too long otherwise you will have a paste.

Serve to spread onto your favorite crackers.

104. Chunky Rocket Spread

Preparation time: 15 minutes
Servings: 1 cup
Ingredients:
1 ½ cup roasted cashew nuts
1 clove garlic
3 cups rocket leaves
¼ Cup Nutritional yeast
¼ Cup extra virgin olive oil
Juice of ½ lemon
Salt & pepper

Preparation:

Place the cashew nuts, garlic and Nutritional yeast into a food processor.

Pulse gently until the nuts are still chunky and mixed well together with the other Ingredients.

Transfer the mix into a bowl.

Place olive oil and lemon juice into the food processor, then add rocket leaves and pulse to blend.

Transfer the rocket mixture into the bowl with the cashews, season with salt and pepper and mix together with a spoon.

Serve with crackers or other low carb breads.

CONCLUSION

There you have it. You are now well on your way to weight the Vegan way!

Be prepared to feel great, have energy you never had before and achieve the weight loss results you always desired! Thank you for taking the time to read my book and stay tuned for more books on Veganism in the future.

Thanks again for your support!

Plant-based high protein cookbook.

Nutrition guide for athletic performance and muscle growth for a strong body while maintaining.

Introduction.

Maybe you got a smart pet and decided you had to go vegan. Maybe you're cutting back on eating beef to lighten your environmental footprint. Whatever the reason, when you reduce meat in your diet, getting enough plant-based protein becomes important.

Why? Every meal should include protein since it contributes to satiety (AKA prevents overeating), provides energy, and helps maintain and build muscle (especially if you're a gym junkie).

The good news; Our food supply is now filled with plant-based protein sources. Hemp and chia seeds weren't sitting on grocery store shelves five years ago; neither were high-quality vegan protein powders. We can now meet our needs without burgers or wings. How to do that in the healthiest way possible? Here's everything you need to know about plant-based protein.

What is plant-based diet?

Plant-based or plant-forward eating patterns focus on foods primarily from plants. This includes not only fruits and vegetables, but also nuts, seeds, oils, whole grains, legumes, and beans. It doesn't mean that you are vegetarian or vegan and never eat meat or dairy. Rather, you are proportionately choosing more of your foods from plant sources.

Mediterranean and vegetarian diets

What is the evidence that plant-based eating patterns are healthy? Much nutrition research has examined plant-based eating patterns such as the Mediterranean diet and a vegetarian diet. The Mediterranean diet has a foundation of plant-based foods; it also includes fish, poultry, eggs, cheese, and yogurt a few times a week, with meats and sweets less often. The Mediterranean diet has been shown in both large population studies and randomized clinical trials to reduce risk of heart disease, metabolic syndrome, diabetes, certain cancers (specifically colon, breast, and prostate cancer), depression, and in older adults, a decreased risk of frailty, along with better mental and physical function.

Vegetarian diets have also been shown to support health, including a lower risk of developing coronary heart disease, high blood pressure, diabetes, and increased longevity. Plant-based diets offer all the necessary protein, fats, carbohydrates, vitamins, and minerals for optimal health, and are often higher in fibre and phytonutrients. However, some vegans may need to add a supplement (specifically vitamin B12) to ensure they receive all the nutrients required.

Vegetarian diet variety.

Vegetarian diets come in lots of shapes and sizes, and you should choose the version that works best for you.

- Semi-vegetarian or flexitarian includes eggs, dairy foods, and occasionally meat, poultry, fish, and seafood.
- Pescatarian includes eggs, dairy foods, fish, and seafood, but no meat or poultry.
- Vegetarian (sometimes referred to as lacto-ovo vegetarian) includes eggs and dairy foods, but no meat, poultry, fish, or seafood.
- Vegan includes no animal foods.

8 WAYS TO GET STARTED WITH A PLANT-BASED DIET

Here are some tips to help you get started on a plant-based diet.

- **Eat lots of vegetables**: Fill half your plate with vegetables at lunch and dinner. Make sure you include plenty of colours in choosing your vegetables. Enjoy vegetables as a snack with hummus, salsa, or guacamole.
- **Change the way you think about meat**: Have smaller amounts. Use it as a garnish instead of a centrepiece.
- **Choose good fats**: Fats in olive oil, olives, nuts and nut butters, seeds, and avocados are particularly healthy choices.
- **Cook a vegetarian meal at least one night a week**: Build these meals around beans, whole grains, and vegetables.
- **Include whole grains for breakfast**: Start with oatmeal, quinoa, buckwheat, or barley. Then add some nuts or seeds along with fresh fruit.
- **Go for greens**: Try a variety of green leafy vegetables such as kale, collards, Swiss chard, spinach, and other greens each day. Steam, grill, braise, or stir-fry to preserve their flavor and nutrients.
- **Build a meal around a salad**: Fill a bowl with salad greens such as romaine, spinach, Bibb, or red leafy greens. Add an assortment of other vegetables along with fresh herbs, beans, peas, or tofu.
- **Eat fruit for dessert**: A ripe, juicy peach, a refreshing slice of watermelon, or a crisp apple will satisfy your craving for a sweet bite after a meal.

INSPIRATION FOR PLANT-BASED EATING THROUGHOUT THE DAY.

Over time, eating a plant-based diet will become second nature. Here are some ideas to get you started.

Breakfast:
- ✓ Rolled oats with walnuts, banana, and a sprinkle of cinnamon.
- ✓ Breakfast wrap: Fill a whole-wheat tortilla with scrambled egg, black beans, peppers, onions, Monterey jack cheese, and a splash of hot sauce or salsa.
- ✓ Whole-wheat English muffin topped with fresh tomato and avocado slices, and blueberries.

Lunch:
- ✓ Greek salad: Chopped mixed greens with fresh tomato, Kalamata olives, fresh parsley, crumbled feta cheese, extra virgin olive oil, and balsamic vinegar. Whole-wheat pita on the side, fresh melon for dessert.
- ✓ Tomato basil soup, whole-grain crackers with tabbouleh, and an apple.
- ✓ Vegetarian pizza topped with mozzarella cheese, tomatoes, broccoli, onions, peppers, and mushroom. Fresh strawberries for dessert.

Dinner:
- ✓ Grilled vegetable kabobs with grilled tofu, and a quinoa and spinach salad.
- ✓ Whole-wheat pasta with cannellini beans and peas, and a romaine salad with cherry tomatoes, dressed with extra virgin olive oil and balsamic vinegar.
- ✓ Vegetarian chili with a spinach-orzo salad.

These ideas are a great way to begin the plant-based dieting, but surely, we have more for you as we go on.

We're increasingly being told about the benefits of including more plant foods in our diets – both for health and sustainability purposes. In this material, we just want to help you all eat a little more goodness every day.

This means eating healthy staples such as vegetables, fruits, starchy carbohydrates, and unless you're following a vegetarian or vegan diet, fish and lean meat. Eating healthily also means taking in a wide variety of plant-based proteins – but what are these, and how can you incorporate them while retaining protein quality?

What plants are high in protein?

Plant protein is simply a meaningful food source of protein which is from plants. This group can include pulses, tofu, soya, tempeh, seitan, nuts, seeds, certain grains and even peas. Pulses are a large group of plants, which include chickpeas, lentils, beans (such as black, kidney and adzuki beans) and split peas.

Plant proteins are highly nutritious – not only as good sources of protein, but also because they provide other nutrients such as fibre, vitamins and minerals. Our intake of fibre tends to be too low, however by incorporating certain plant proteins into your diet, such as pulses, peas and nuts, you can easily boost your fibre intake. Did you know that our peas, soya beans and green beans are all a great source of plant fibre?

Why Protein is Important.

Protein is a vital nutrient responsible for the growth, maintenance and repair of our bodies. So, we must ensure we eat enough high-quality protein every day to keep our bodies healthy. Essentially, protein is fundamental to the basic structure of our body.

There are 9 essential amino acids, and when you eat a protein source containing all of these it is called a 'complete' protein. Animal protein sources are complete, and they include fish, poultry such as chicken and red meat.

Plant sources of protein, with the exception of soya and quinoa, are 'incomplete'. This is because plant protein sources tend to lack at least 1 of the 9 essential amino acids. So how can you ensure that you consume all of the essential amino acids when eating plant proteins? The answer is protein combining.

What is protein combining?

Put simply, protein combining means eating a selection of incomplete plant protein sources, to ensure you consume all of the essential amino acids. As a general rule of thumb, pulses and grains lack different essential amino acids. So, eating a pulse and a grain provides an overall complete protein source.

With this in mind, it's easy to get all the essential amino acids your body needs. For example, a serving of rice and peas or bread and hummus would give you a complete protein source. And remember, you needn't eat your combined proteins in just one meal – they can be eaten at different points during the day or even the week!

Starting a plant-based diet for your optimum health.

Diets centred on a wide variety of plant foods offer affordable, tasty and nutritious options. Plant-based diets which are rich in beans, nuts, seeds, fruit and vegetables, whole grains such as oats, rice, and cereal based foods such as breads, and pasta can provide all the nutrients needed for good health. This includes essential fats, protein, vitamins, minerals and plenty of fibre too.

Well balanced plant-based diets that are also low in saturated fat, can help you manage your weight and may reduce your risk of type 2 diabetes, cardiovascular disease and some cancers. However, as with any diet, plant-based nutrition needs to be planned.

Most nutrients are abundantly available in plant-based diets, but if you are avoiding all or minimising your consumption of animal-derived foods there are a few nutrients that you need to pay attention to.

Calcium: Calcium is essential for bone health, along with weight bearing exercise and a healthy diet. An adult requires approximately 700mg per day. Dairy foods are rich in calcium but if you are not eating these make sure you obtain calcium from other sources like fortified plant based dairy alternatives, dried fruit e.g. figs, nuts such as almonds, leafy green vegetables, red kidney beans, sesame seeds, tahini and tofu to lower your risk of bone fractures.

Omega 3 fatty acids: These fats have been shown to be important for health and are commonly found in oily fish. However, if you are not eating fish, plant sources of omega 3 include walnuts, flax (linseed), hemp seeds, chia seeds and soya beans. Oils such as hemp, rapeseed and flaxseed oil provide essential omega 3 fats and are preferable to corn/sunflower oils.

Vitamin D: Vitamin D is needed to keep bones, teeth and muscles healthy and is made in our bodies when our skin is exposed to appropriate sunlight. In the UK this is usually between April and September. During the winter months, we need to get vitamin D from our diet because the sun isn't strong enough for the body to make it.

Plant-based sources of vitamin D include sun-exposed mushrooms and fortified foods such as vegetable spreads, breakfast cereals and plant based dairy alternatives. Since it's difficult to get enough vitamin D from food alone, everyone should consider taking a daily supplement of 10mcg/ day during the autumn and winter months. Some vitamin D supplements are not suitable for vegans. Vitamin D2 and lichen-derived vitamin D3 are suitable.

Iodine: The major sources of iodine in our diet are dairy products and fish. The iodine content of plant foods depends on the iodine content of the soil which is variable. Foods grown closer to the ocean tend to be higher in iodine. Where soils are iodine deficient, iodised salt and seaweed provide iodine which is needed in moderation. As the iodine content of seaweed is variable, and sometimes too high, guidance is not to consume sea vegetables more than once a week. An excess of iodine is also unhealthy so if you are taking a supplement, discuss this with your dietician.

Vitamin B12: We need vitamin B12 for many reasons. Too little can result in fatigue, anaemia and nerve damage and increase homo-cysteine levels leading to cardiovascular disease. Most people get vitamin B12 by eating animal products. If you are eliminating all animal derived foods, the only reliable sources of vitamin B12 are fortified foods and supplements. Suitable B12-fortified foods include some breakfast cereals, yeast extracts, soya yoghurts and non-dairy milks. To make sure you get enough vitamin B12, either eat fortified foods at least twice a day, aiming for 3mcg of vitamin B12 a day, or take a supplement, 10mcg daily or at least 2000mcg weekly. If you are worried whether you are obtaining sufficient vitamin B12, a dietician can calculate your intake from food/supplements or a doctor can check your blood homo-cysteine levels.

Iron: Plant sources of iron include dried fruits, whole grains, nuts, green leafy vegetables, seeds and pulses. The form of iron in plant foods is absorbed far less efficiently compared to iron from animal derived sources such as meat and eggs. Eat plenty of fruits and vegetables rich in vitamin C to help the iron to be absorbed e.g. citrus fruits, strawberries, green leafy vegetables and peppers.

Zinc: Phytates found in plant foods such as whole grains and beans reduce zinc absorption, so it's important to eat good sources of zinc-containing foods. Eat fermented soya such as tempeh and miso; beans (soak dried beans then rinse before cooking to increase zinc absorption); whole grains; nuts; seeds and some fortified breakfast cereals.

Selenium: Plant sources of this mineral include grains, seeds and nuts. Just two Brazil nuts daily will provide you with your daily requirement of selenium.

Protein: Plant-based sources of protein include lentils, beans, chickpeas, seeds, nuts and nut butters (e.g. peanut butter), and tofu. Eggs, and dairy are also good sources if you are eating these. Meat substitutes like vegetarian burgers, soya sausages, and other meat alternatives can be useful for those adapting to a plant-based diet and can provide a source of protein. However, as with any processed foods, these can often be high in salt and fat so should be used in moderation. These products may contain animal ingredients such as eggs, milk derivatives and honey so careful label reading is necessary if you wish to follow a vegan diet.

It's a warm reminder that, well-planned plant-based diets can support healthy living at every age and life-stage. Include a wide variety of healthy whole foods to ensure your diet is balanced and sustainable. Eat your veggies! Compared to the average Western diet, plant-based diets are rich in everything you've been told to eat more of: fibre from fruits and vegetables, and fats from nuts and seeds—while generally low in the saturated fat that animal-based foods can be rich in.

Soaking methods and cooking.

Whenever "soaking" is mentioned, we "think" beans and that's correct. We know that beans is one of the most potent source of protein and contains fractions of other nutrients too as recently confirmed by health experts.

Beans are the musical fruit, the more you eat the more you...well, toot. Let's face it, beans are yummy. But the gas sucks. So to keep your beans more tasty and less musical it's always a good idea to learn about the best methods for soaking beans. Soaking beans is not hard. Sure, it may take a few hours but it's not like you have to stand there watching them get submerged. Just be sure to plan a little ahead of time when making recipes calling for dried beans or legumes.

Soaking your beans helps them cook faster and more evenly, and it can also make them easier to digest. If you add salt to the soaking water (in other words, make a brine), your beans will cook even faster; the salt helps break down their skins. Here are a few methods; choose the one that best fits your schedule. And keep in mind that you never need to soak legumes like lentils or split peas.

To help make the most of your frugal and yummy bean meals I've summarized three easy methods for soaking beans, they are: the long soak method (where you soak beans overnight), the quick soak method, and the quick cook method.

The Long Soak

The "Long Soak" method is the most common way to soak your beans. Just put your beans in a large bowl or pot of water and let them sit submerged for 8-12 hours overnight. Soaking beans overnight actually begins bean germination and promotes enzyme release. The germination process is what breaks down all the complex bean sugars. Breaking down the complex sugar is a good thing as this is what gives us gas. Apparently, soaking beans overnight using the "Long Soak" method can reduce complex sugars by up to 60 percent. I usually use this method of soaking dried beans with exceptional results – no gastrointestinal gusts.

Quick Soaking Beans (The Power Soak).

I have tried the "Quick Soaking Beans or Power Soak" method a few times. But basically, just bring a pot of water to boil, add your beans, and then let them boil for about three minutes. After boiling, remove the beans from the stove and let them sit in the hot water for 2-6 hours. This method apparently removes 80 percent of complex bean sugars. How does that toot your horn?

Quick Cook

While bigger beans like red beans, chick peas, and navy beans do require soaking – some smaller beans and legumes require little to no soaking. Legumes like lentils, mung beans, or split peas can be added to soup (like lentil soup) without ever needing time soaked in water before cooking. If you're using smaller beans and legumes, then use the "Quick Cook" or "no soak method" where you just throw your dried beans into a pot and cook it till you're satisfied with its degree of softness. I wouldn't recommend the "Quick Cook" method for tougher beans like kidney or chick peas cause you'll have a lot of gas and may not feel your stomach normally for a couple of days.

More on beans soaking and cooking.

Easy, forgiving, healthy and economical, beans are a home cook's secret weapon. Yes, canned beans are convenient, but knowing how to cook dried beans gives you flexibility, and makes for a far more delicious meal.

A few handy tips:

- Check for a date on the beans; freshness matters. Dried beans last up to two years, but are best cooked within a year of harvest. Always rinse beans before cooking, and check for stray rocks, twigs and leaves.
- Leave substantial time for bean soaking (either overnight or using our shortcut method) and cooking. If you are short on time, choose lentils or adzuki beans, which cook quickly and don't need soaking.
- To add more flavour, consider cooking your beans in stock or broth instead of water.

Choosing Your Bean

There are dozens of varieties of beans, but these are the ones you're most likely to encounter. Use this list to figure out what to buy when you want them to fall apart into a soup or dal (lentils, flageolet and split peas), or hold their shape for salads (adzuki, black-eyed peas, chickpeas, cranberry and kidney). As a general rule, 1 cup dried beans make about 3 cups cooked.

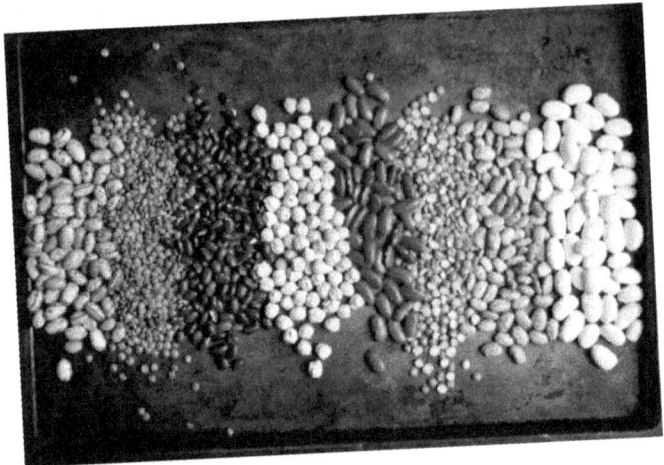

Above, from left: cranberry beans, lentils, black beans, chickpeas, red kidney beans, split peas, pinto beans and cannellini beans.

Adzuki: These small, scarlet beans cook quickly, with a sweet flavour. They're often used in Japanese bean paste desserts, but are versatile enough for salads, soups and stews.

Black: Also known as turtle beans, these full-flavored beans are classic in Latin American cooking, usually for soups and stews.

Black-eyed peas: These small earthy-flavoured beans, also known as Crowder peas and cowpeas, are particularly cherished in Southern cooking.

Cannellini: These mild, starchy white beans are often used in soups and stews, particularly in Italian cooking.

Chickpeas: These nutty-tasting legumes, also known as garbanzo beans, are used all the globe in many guises: soups, stews, dips and even fried or roasted as a snack.

Cranberry: These red-and-brown speckled beans have a rich, toasty flavour. They hold their shape well for salads, soups and stews.

Fava: Dried favas, also known as broad beans, have a very strong, meaty flavour and a somewhat thick skin. Beloved in Middle Eastern cuisine, they are made into soups, stews and salads.

Flageolet: These are a creamy, smooth, pale green-to-white-hued bean from France with a thin skin. They work well for soups and purées.

Great Northern: These large white beans with a firm texture and gentle, nutty flavour are great for stews and soups.

Kidney: These large red beans are often used in salads and chili. Some people find them particularly hard to digest, but soaking and rinsing before cooking can help, as does using a pressure cooker.

*Lentils***:** There are several varieties of these tiny legumes, ranging from shiny black beluga lentils, which remain nicely intact for salads, to orange-hued "red" lentils, which collapse into a thick purée when simmered. In between, there are brown lentils (good all-purpose lentils) and more expensive French green lentils, also called Puy lentils, which take a bit longer to cook and have a nice sweet flavour. All lentils are relatively quick-cooking and don't need any pre-soaking.

Lima: Large white dried lima beans take on a velvety, creamy texture after simmering, and hold their shape well.

Navy: These small white beans have a nutty flavour, and cook more quickly than other white beans. They are the traditional choice for Boston baked beans. Like red kidney beans, they can be easier to digest if you soak and rinse before cooking.

Pinto: These are small brownish-pink beans frequently used in Mexican and other Latin American cooking, particularly for refried beans, stews and chili.

Split peas: Green or yellow split peas are small legumes often used in soups, and in the case of the yellow ones, Indian dals. They do not need to be soaked before cooking.

Seasoning

You can simmer beans and other legumes in nothing but plain water with salt and get great results. But before you start cooking, take a minute to add the herbs, spices, stock and aromatics that make beans even better. Even a humble onion and a bay leaf works wonders.

There's a myth out regarding beans and salt — specifically, that you should never salt your beans before cooking because the salt keeps them from cooking through.

That's just not true. You can add salt to your bean pot at the beginning of cooking, and your beans will be better seasoned for it.

If you've ever cooked beans for hours without them softening, it's probably because you're using old beans, or you've got hard (mineral-rich) water, or there's an acidic ingredient in the pot, which can slow down cooking. Using distilled water solves the hard water problem. (And soaking your beans in salt water before cooking not only adds flavour, it can also help them cook more quickly.)

Don't stop at salt and black pepper. Spices like cumin, cinnamon, coriander, ground chilies and allspice add depth and complexity to your bean pot and are traditional additions in many cultures. To give spices a richer character, toast them in the pot for a few minutes until you can smell them, then add beans and liquid.

Cooking

You've soaked your beans (or maybe not) and they're ready for some heat. Simmering them on the stove is the time-honoured method, and I'll tell you how to do it. But you can also cook them in a slow cooker or a pressure cooker — whatever you prefer.

STOVETOP METHOD

Place your beans in your pot and cover them with at least 2 inches of water, and turn the heat to low. Stir them gently and occasionally, never letting them hit a strong boil; this can burst their skins and make them mushy or unevenly cooked. Depending upon the variety, dried beans will cook quickly (about 15 minutes for red lentils) or slowly (up to 3 to 4 hours for un-soaked chickpeas or lima beans).

SLOW-COOKER METHOD

To use a slow cooker, cover your beans with 2 inches of water or broth and salt to taste, and toss any aromatics you like into the pot. Set your machine to the low setting and cook until the beans are done, usually 3 to 6 hours. If you are cooking kidney beans, you need to boil them on the stove for 10 minutes first before adding them to the slow cooker. This makes them much more digestible.

PRESSURE-COOKER METHOD

To cook beans in a pressure cooker, place your soaked or un-soaked beans with enough water to cover by 2 inches into the pressure cooker. Add salt, any aromatics you like, and a tablespoon of neutral oil to help keep the foam from clogging the vent. Make sure not to exceed the maximum fill line for your brand of pressure cooker. This is usually around the halfway mark for beans. Cook at high pressure for anywhere from 5 to 10 minutes for small beans such as black-eyed peas, lentils and split peas, to up to 35 to 40 minutes for larger beans such as chickpeas. Soaked beans will cook more quickly than un-soaked beans.

Testing for Doneness

How do you know when your beans are ready to eat? Read on for the signs that it's time to taste — and don't toss that cooking liquid.

To make sure your beans are cooked thoroughly, scoop up a couple of beans and blow on them. The skin should curl and wrinkle. Then taste. They are done when they're tender and cooked through to the centre (but not mushy). Let them cool in their cooking liquid.

A tip: Don't throw out your bean cooking liquid, that tasty pot liquor. Salt it if need be, and save it. It's basically a rich vegetarian stock that freezes well for up to six months; use it as you would any other chicken or vegetable stock.

Would you like one of my favourite recipes? I bet you would! Here you go:

Simple Pinto Beans.

Pinto beans are emblematic of the Old West — good cheap hearty fare. These plain ones are good with just about anything or as a meal in a tin plate, cowboy-style, with a chunk of cornbread. For the best tasting beans, cook at a bare simmer, and keep the liquid level just 1 inch above the beans' surface as they cook.

Ingredient: 1-pound pinto beans, 1 small onion, halved, 1 bay leaf, ¾ pound slab bacon, 1 tablespoon kosher salt, 1 tablespoon paprika, ¼ teaspoon cayenne.

Preparation: Pick over the beans for small rocks or debris. Rinse well, then cover with cold water and soak for 6 hours or overnight. Transfer beans to a soup pot and add water to cover by 1 inch. Add onion, bay leaf and bacon and bring to a boil. Reduce heat to a bare simmer, partly cover pot with lid, and cook for 1 hour, stirring occasionally.

Stir in salt, paprika and cayenne, then continue simmering until beans are soft and creamy and the broth is well seasoned and lightly thickened, about 1 hour more. Remove bacon and chop roughly, then return to pot. (Dish may be prepared up to 2 days ahead.)

Enjoy the treat!

Storage

How and where you store your beans, lentils and more, both before and after cooking, can dramatically affect flavour and texture. Store uncooked dried beans in a dark, cool cabinet for up to a year. They really go downhill after two years, so throw out all your old beans, especially if you can't remember when you bought them. If you can find a harvest date on your package of beans, all the better. Some beans may have been stored in a warehouse for months or even a year before they arrive at your market.

Cooked beans are best stored in their cooking liquid in the refrigerator for up to 5 days. Or drain the beans and toss them with a little oil, salt and pepper (or a vinaigrette) before chilling. This both preserves them and flavours them. Beans can turn mushy in the freezer, but if you do want to try to freeze them, do so in their cooking liquid.

The plant-base athlete.

Have you ever wondered if athletes can succeed eating plant-based or if your physical performance will plummet if you eat fewer animal foods? I myself am by no means an athlete but I am well-versed in plant-based nutrition and know that athletes can thrive on a plant food if they wish. It does take a little extra planning (and as most athletes know, no matter your dietary preferences, you need to be mindful about how you feed your body before, during and after an event or tough training session).

So, whether you're decreasing or ditching animal foods for ethical, environmental or health reasons, or just want to see what all the fuss is about with plant-based eating, I hope you learn some valuable strategies as we go on!

To provide top-notch information I interviewed my friend, long-time vegan and plant-based nutrition expert Matt Ruscigno, MPH, RD. Matt co-authored the books No Meat Athlete and Plant-Based Sports Nutrition and founded Vegan Nutrition Consulting, a network of nutrition experts to provide science-based vegan nutrition education for both individuals and corporate wellness. He's also done some extreme endurance events and knows first-hand what it's like to fuel for intense activity. I also chatted with a female plant-based athlete who's experienced some cool changes in her performance since tweaking her eating pattern. Now let's get into it!

Can Athletes Succeed While Eating Plant-Based?

Whether you're simply eating more plant foods or going vegan, there is lots of evidence to support plant-based eating for optimal athletic performance. According to the Vegetarian Nutrition Dietetic Practice Group of the Academy of Nutrition and Dietetics, "*Vegetarian diets are linked to decreased risk for chronic diseases including cardiovascular disease, type 2 diabetes, and certain cancers, while their naturally high carbohydrate and phytochemical content may help athletes optimize their training, performance and recovery.*"

In other words, you're more likely to experience benefits from this style of eating than disadvantages. As long as you're meeting your fuelling needs and eating satisfying foods, a plant-based eating style can support your sports performance and your overall health!

Amanda Wagner, who is a plant-based athlete and nutrition student, said that her performance and recovery has improved since switching to a plant-based eating style. She even qualified for the Boston Marathon while eating vegan! Now if that's not a successful athlete, I don't know what is. *"I'm training for my second marathon now on a vegan diet and feeling the best I've felt in years and running personal bests in all my races so far this summer. I am confident my vegan diet has played a key role in my strong athletic performances this year,"* she says.

How do Athletes Get the Nutrients They Need from Plant-Based Foods?

No matter your eating style, carbohydrates are key for fuelling workouts. You're probably familiar with carb-rich plant-based foods including grains, potatoes and fruit. It's not tough to get enough carbs while eating plant-based! Sometimes all the fibre in plant foods can fill you up too fast and it's OK to eat some refined grains such as white pasta and white rice.

Many of us have been trained to believe that we need protein from meat, dairy and eggs to maintain strong muscles and bones. In actuality, plant foods can provide all the amino acids and protein we need! Protein-rich plant foods include beans, lentils, nuts and soy foods such as tofu and tempeh. Bonus: these foods tend to be way more affordable than animal-based protein foods!

Another concern about plant-based eating as an athlete may be getting enough calories. While it's true that vegetables are low in calories, there are calorie-dense foods in the plant kingdom including nuts, seeds, avocados and olives. *"Nuts and seeds and nut and seed butters are crucial for athletes. And there's no shame in so-called 'processed foods' like veggie burgers and vegan meats,"* Matt says.

"Try to cook whenever possible, but do not shy away from packaged vegan foods, frozen dinners, or restaurant meals as they can help you fill your daily vegan athlete plate," Amanda says. She echoes Matt's sentiments about processed foods and incorporates protein bars and powders into her day for an extra boost, especially during heavy training periods.

Beyond the macronutrients (carbs, protein, fat), athletes also need to be mindful of certain micronutrients (vitamins and minerals). According to Matt, "Iron should be on the mind of all athletes, especially plant-based and vegan ones. Fortunately, plenty of plant foods have iron and absorption is increased by combining them with vitamin-C containing foods. This pairing happens naturally — salsa in burritos, tomatoes in falafel sandwiches and bell peppers in tofu scrambles."

Keep in mind that women need more iron than men so this is a nutrient that females of child-bearing age (or anyone who menstruates) need to be mindful of. I recommend asking your health care provider to check your iron status when you go in for your yearly check-up (yes, you should be going in for those yearly visits, and not just for your lady bits!). It involves a simple blood draw and an inexpensive lab test. This is for all females, not just those who are eating plant-based or who are active (but especially if you fall into these categories).

How Can Athletes Get Started with Plant-Based Eating?

Think substitution rather than elimination. Substitute meat with tofu, tempeh, beans and lentils. Substitute dairy-based milk, cheese and yogurt with fortified plant-based versions of these foods. Hopefully you're already eating a wide variety of colourful vegetables and fruits, but if you're not, make it a goal to add at least two different colours of produce to every meal! Colours in vegetables and fruits represent different nutrients which are crucial for fuelling and recovery.

You'll also need to do some additions along with your substitutions. I love adding baked tofu to pasta for a protein boost of an otherwise carb-centric meal. And trying some legume-based pastas for even more of a boost. Adding peanut butter to smoothies is great for adding protein, fat and calories. Avocado in salads and wraps is another great way to add fat, calories and deliciousness to plant-based meals. And remember that it's OK to cook with oils such as olive oil. Just because you're eating plant-based doesn't mean you need to start overly restricting certain foods.

Looking for specific ideas for plant-based meals and snacks? *"Bean dips are so good! In taste and for easy, quick calories and protein. You can eat them with fresh veggies, on sandwiches, with a spoon, in sauces — the application is unlimited. And there's more than hummus! I make white bean and black bean dips regularly,"* Matt says.

Some of Amanda's favourite meals are pasta with kidney beans and vegetables; black beans, rice, and vegetables; and tofu and vegetable stir-fry. "You do have to eat a greater volume of food as a vegan athlete, but it does not have to be annoying. Make it fun by trying as many new meals and snacks as your time and budget will allow," she says.

Have fun with it, experiment with different recipes and enjoy the taste and benefits of plant-based eating! For personalized guidance on food, nutrition and dietary supplements, consider working with a registered dietician nutritionist who specializes in plant-based nutrition.

HANDY TIPS AS A PLANT-BASED ATHLETE.

If you have been inspired by the knowledge here so far, and adopted a whole-food, plant-based diet as your foundation for health, perhaps you are ready to pursue meaningful fitness goals but don't know where to start. Or perhaps you have been working out for a long time and are concerned that your new diet will affect your performance. With the knowledge and relationship, I've gathered from as many plant-based athlete, I've sorted through all of the issues unique to vegan athletes and guided thousands to successfully incorporate physical activity into their vegan lifestyle routine. Here are some of my top tips:

- ✓ **Unlearn the Most Common Nutrition Myth**— a common question that comes up among many people new to a plant-based diet is, "what do I eat?" What to avoid on a plant-based it quite clear: all animal products. If we want that plant-based diet to be a healthy one, we take things a step farther, also eliminating processed foods, including oils and refined carbohydrates. But knowing only what not to eat leaves many wondering how to get adequate nutrition, especially protein. The human requirement for protein is so low (5 to 10 percent of our total caloric intake) that as long as you consume adequate calories to maintain your weight, it is virtually impossible to have a protein deficiency. Further, if you are eating nothing but a variety of whole, natural plants, you will get enough of every single essential amino acid, regardless of which foods you choose (the complete protein myth has long been debunked). You would experience a calorie deficiency before a protein deficiency, and

both are virtually non-existent in first-world societies.
- ✓ **_Know Which Foods Best Fuel Your Fitness_**— Nobody is fuelled by kale, so don't fool yourself into thinking you will get sufficient energy to perform athletic activities from leafy greens and other non-starchy vegetables (which average about 100 and 150 calories per pound, respectively). For long-lasting fuel, vegan athletes and non-athletes alike need to centre their diets around the more calorically dense whole plant foods that are rich in complex carbohydrates such as potatoes, beans, lentils, squash, brown rice, oats, quinoa, and other starchy vegetables, legumes, and grains (which range from about 350 to 600 calories per pound). Fruits (which average about 250 calories per pound) are also an excellent source of fuel. This is especially true right before exercise, because they digest quickly and will not weigh heavily in your stomach during cardiovascular exercise. When you consume an abundance of whole, unprocessed plant foods, you get not only get the fuel, but also the full range of macronutrients (protein, fat, carbohydrates, water, and fibre) and micronutrients (vitamins, minerals, enzymes, antioxidants, and other important phytochemicals). Since most whole plant foods contain 600 or fewer calories per pound (with the exception of nuts and seeds, which range from 2,500 to 3,000 calories per pound, on average), you can eat a lot of food, experiencing many flavours and textures, and the volume will fill you up before you overdose on calories. Overeating is easy to do when consuming refined and processed foods. By consuming foods high in nutrients and low in calorie density, you can support energy

production and muscle recovery without excess fat gain, while avoiding the energy-sucking process of digesting refined foods.
- ✓ **Eat Many Small Meals per Day**— when it comes to what to eat, know that your options are boundless, with ample varieties of fruits, vegetables, legumes, grains, nuts, and seeds. Because whole plant foods are lower in calorie density (see #2), you may find that you need to eat more volume than you did before. Simply choose the foods you like the most and eat 5 or 6 small meals throughout the day until you are comfortably full. This way, you'll find it easier not to under- or overeat. You will have sufficient fuel to work out any time, rather than finding yourself too hungry, too full, or too tired to exercise, as is common when we eat three more substantial meals each day. The two biggest obstacles that keep people from exercising regularly are shortages of time and energy. You can now put the energy issue to rest and work on time management to ensure that regular exercise is part of your routine. If you aren't losing or gaining weight as you'd like, then it's a good idea to get a general sense of how many calories you need to eat in a day. To determine your own personal caloric needs, simply use an online Harris-Benedict calculator, and enter five simple bits of data. This will reveal two numbers: (1) your estimated BMR (basal metabolic rate), the average number of calories you would burn if you slept all day and (2) your daily calorie needs, taking into account your activity level.
- ✓ **Get Moving ... and Have Fun**! — Over the years, one thing I have discovered to be profoundly true is that if it isn't fun, I am unlikely to do it regularly. This clearly applies to fitness. If your current

exercise routine is not enjoyable, you will find yourself consciously or unconsciously avoiding exercise by finding other ways to occupy your time, such as putting in extra hours at work or distracting yourself with entertainment or hobbies. This approach will not lead to fitness success. To succeed, you will need to find genuine enjoyment in whatever activity you choose. Exercise is not just putting on spandex and grunting while lifting weights. Exercise is hiking, swimming, jogging, playing team sports, and anything else that increases your heart rate, gets your body moving vigorously, and puts stress on your muscles. Find a physical activity you enjoy, and do it regularly. I suggest exercising for 30 to 90 minutes a day, three to five days per week, which allows at least a couple of days off for recovery.

ENERGY AND PERFORMANCE.

Whether training for a local 10 km run or the Euro 2020 Championship, athletes of all shapes, sizes and levels share a common goal: to perform to the best of their ability. Technical expertise and training are the cornerstones of improving athletic performance, but good nutrition is equally crucial for success. Over the last two decades, our understanding of the important role that dietary protein plays in muscle building and recovery has grown vastly. We now know that it is not simply the quantity of protein consumed, but also the quality of that protein and when we consume it that dictates muscle health and function.

- **Adequate does not mean optimal**— the daily recommended allowance (RDA) for protein is 0.8 grams per kilogram of body weight per day, which translates to 56 g for a 70 kg/178-pound man.

The vast majority of people consuming a typical western style diet easily achieve this level. But at Kerry's recent Scientific Advisory Council Meeting, Professor Stuart Phillips, Director of the Centre for Nutrition, Exercise, and Health Research at McMaster University, warned that RDAs are minimum levels set to prevent deficiency rather than levels that will optimise health. Protein has countless functions in the human body; however, it is especially important for the maintenance and recovery of muscle. Muscle health is a critical determinant of athletic performance, so, for athletes, achieving optimal rather than merely adequate protein intake is key. Intense exercise causes the proteins that make up muscle to be broken down. This damage is responsible for muscle soreness and can ultimately reduce strength and function if the proteins are not replenished. Consuming protein in the diet can offset this effect. Eating a high protein meal decreases muscle breakdown and increases muscle repair and synthesis (Moore D et al., 2015). As a result, the American College of Sports Medicine advocates protein intakes higher than the RDA. Individuals who take part in endurance sports (runners, cyclists, swimmers) are advised to consume between 1.2 – 1.4 g per kg body weight per day (84-98 g per day for a 70 kg/178 pound man) while for power disciplines (strength or speed) intakes of up to 1.7g per kg body weight per day (119 g/d) are recommended.

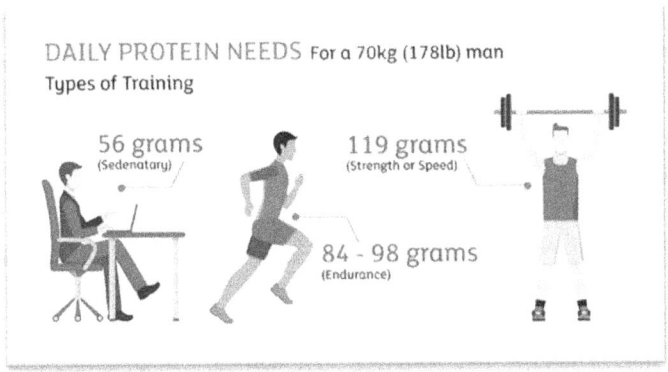

- **Quality Matters**— it's not just the amount of protein, but also the type of protein in the diet that athletes need to take note of. Scientific research shows that simply consuming enough protein will not optimise muscle repair and synthesis because not all types of protein are equally beneficial. In order to utilise the protein, we eat, the body breaks it down into basic building blocks, called amino acids. The source of the protein influences our ability to digest it properly and, therefore, the availability of these crucial building blocks. Protein from plants such as vegetables, nuts, seeds, grains, and legumes are not as well digested as protein from animal sources or soy protein. In addition, not all proteins contain all of the amino acids the human body needs. Some amino acids, called essential amino acids, cannot be produced by the human body and must be consumed in the diet. Most plant proteins lack one or more of these essential amino acids, meaning plant sources must be combined in the diet to provide for the body's needs. Egg, milk and soy proteins are highly digestible and contain all of the essential amino acids, meaning they are considered the highest quality proteins for humans. Recent scientific research has allowed us to refine this list even further for athletes because when it comes to building muscle, one specific amino acid, leucine, plays a critical role (Layman D et al., 2015). Leucine acts like a molecular switch that turns on the body's machinery for manufacturing muscle. Whey protein contains more leucine than any other source of protein and clinical studies have shown that whey stimulates muscle synthesis more effectively than other high-quality proteins, especially when consumed after exercise. As a result, whey protein recovery supplements have become extremely popular.

- **Timing is of the essence**— Focusing on post-exercise whey supplementation is only part of a bigger picture. Optimal muscle repair and synthesis will not be achieved simply by drinking a protein shake after a workout. Frequent training is required to improve performance. As a result, muscle breakdown, repair and synthesis become an ongoing process and regular intake of high-quality protein is needed. We now know that consuming around 20-30g of protein can "switch on" muscle protein synthesis, but this effect plateaus when more protein is consumed (Moore D et al., 2015). This means that consuming larger amounts of protein at that same meal offers no additional benefit. For this reason, spreading protein intake throughout the day, such that 20-30g of high-quality protein is consumed at breakfast, lunch and dinner, is more beneficial. This type of meal pattern will lead to more muscle synthesis and less muscle breakdown throughout the day. A recent study carried out by researchers at Maastricht University in the Netherlands suggests that one additional snack before sleeping may further optimise muscle synthesis (Snijders T et al., 2015). Sleep is crucial, not only for athletic performance but also for general health and wellness. The hours we spend sleeping, however, constitute a period of fasting and this leaves the body vulnerable to muscle breakdown. The researchers found that consuming 20-30g of high quality protein before bed minimised muscle break down and promoted muscle synthesis during sleep, meaning that a protein packed bedtime snack could be beneficial.

What does all of this mean in terms of diet?

Thanks to our improved understanding of the way in which dietary protein affects muscle health, we can now define not just the quantity of protein, but also the quality and timing of intake needed to optimise muscle recovery and function, and ultimately, performance.

1. **Quantity**: RDAs for protein are minimum rather than optimum levels. To maximize muscle health target 1.2-1.7g per kg of body weight per day
2. **Quality**: As you are a vegetarian, combine plant sources of protein to ensure your body gets all of the essential amino acids.
3. **Timing**: It is important to consume protein regularly throughout the day. Aim to include 20-30g of high-quality protein at breakfast, lunch, dinner and as a bedtime snack.

Six reasons you'd want to embrace the plant-based diet as an athlete.

- Even athletes are at risk for heart disease: In one study, 44 percent of endurance cyclists and runners had coronary plaques. A plant-based diet keeps athletes' hearts strong by reversing plaque, bringing down blood pressure and cholesterol, and reducing weight.

- Meat consumption and high cholesterol levels exacerbate inflammation, which can result in pain and impair athletic performance and recovery. Studies show that a plant-based diet may have an anti-inflammatory effect.
- A plant-based diet, which is low in saturated fat and free of cholesterol, helps improve blood viscosity, or thickness. That helps more oxygen reach the muscles, which improves athletic performance.
- Plant-based diets improve arterial flexibility and diameter, leading to better blood flow. One study found that even a single high-fat meal, including sausage and egg McMuffins, impaired arterial function for several hours.
- Compared with meat-eaters, people eating a plant-based diet get more antioxidants, which help neutralize free radicals. Free radicals lead to muscle fatigue, reduced athletic performance, and impaired recovery.
- Plant-based diets, which are typically low in fat and high in fibre, can reduce body fat. Reduced body fat is associated with increased aerobic capacity—or the ability to use oxygen to fuel exercise. Studies show that athletes on a plant-based diet increase their VO2 max—the maximum amount of oxygen they can use during intense exercise—leading to better endurance.

Let's Put the Protein Myth to Rest

The idea that plant sources are insufficient to meet protein requirements is an outdated myth. The Academy of Nutrition and Dietetics supports the notion that an appropriately planned vegan or vegetarian diet can meet the energy and macronutrient needs (including protein) of athletes.

But the key words here are appropriately planned. Meeting your protein needs as a vegan athlete isn't rocket science, but it may take a little effort or at least forethought.

- Eat a variety of foods throughout the day.
- Include high-lysine foods when possible.
- Know roughly how many grams you need and plan accordingly.

While the protein question may never go away completely, at least you know you can be healthy and reach your goals.

And now you know the science to prove it.

Protein and recovery.

Recovery after exercise is just as important (if not more) than the exercises you do while you're working out. The body can only run off what we give it, and what we give it determines our health in more ways than one. After exercise, the body needs to be refuelled with a delicate mix of protein and carbohydrates from quality foods. Not cheap protein shakes, fast food, processed bars, or junk food. Good, clean food is what it needs. Muscles can utilize these foods better than anything else, and these foods are better for our blood sugar which should be considered post-workout too.

What Happens in the Body Post-Workout?

After we workout, our cortisol levels are normally high while insulin is usually low. This happens because we've put stress on the body which then causes stress hormones to pump out more abundantly in the body (namely cortisol) and insulin levels drop because glucose has been depleted which lowers blood sugar levels. This might be one reason you feel so hungry after you work out and are more likely to just grab something to help yourself feel better. Blood sugar should be managed by eating something that will provide quality carbohydrates to the body, but also to allow those carbs to enter in rapidly into the bloodstream so they can help reach muscle cells and replenish muscle glycogen stores. The key is not to choose refined carbs, but whole food-based carbs.

We all know eating well is essential for a healthy lifestyle. Getting the right nutrients affects everything from your mood and risk of injury and illness, to your weight and even how you look.

A good diet for any regular exerciser should be made up of a good balance of macronutrients: healthy carbohydrates to provide energy and fuel your training; fats to provide energy and support cell growth; and lean protein to help rebuild and recover. When you're asking your body to do things like 4-hour bike rides or 26.2-mile runs, getting enough protein becomes a key focus, to help your body's cells and tissues – such as muscle – recover, repair and grow.

Protein is made up of 20 different organic compounds known as amino acids. While some of these amino acids are made by our bodies, there are nine – known as essential amino acids – the body doesn't create. These have to be provided through diet.

Studies have shown that leucine – a branch chain amino acid (BCAA) found in protein-rich foods and not created by the body – is particularly important as it's one of the key drivers of muscle protein synthesis. To put that in simpler terms, it helps you build muscle mass. Leucine is used by muscles as fuel and so is depleted after exercise.

While leucine is found in many animal-based proteins such as chicken, eggs, beef and whey it's also found in a number of plant-based foods. Vegan foods high in leucine include soybeans, hemp seeds, peanuts, almonds, oats and soy and pea protein powders. Vegan or non-vegan, to supercharge your recovery you should be aiming to eat some form of protein and carbohydrate – to replace the energy used by your body – within two hours of exercising and ideally within the first 45 minutes.

How does your body get protein from vegan diets?

The body gets protein from a vegan diet in the same way it does from a diet that includes animal products, by eating protein-rich foods. You may have heard a theory that you need to combine plant-based protein types to ensure you're getting a 'complete' protein but luckily, that complicated concept has been disproved.

Complete vs. incomplete proteins: the latest thinking

All animal proteins contain each of the nine essential amino acids and are termed 'complete protein', some plant-based proteins are deficient in certain amino acids, leading these to be termed 'incomplete'.

This labelling promotes the thinking that you'd need to combine different plant-based proteins in one sitting to ensure you got enough of each amino acid, but the reality is that as long as you're eating a variety of different proteins on a regular basis, your body will be able to pull from this pool of amino acids as it needs.

There are also a number of plant-based proteins including quinoa, hemp seeds, soy, and chia seeds which contain all nine essential amino acids in roughly equal amounts.

How much protein do I actually need to consume?

According to the British Nutrition Foundation, the protein requirements of a normal adult are 0.75g per kilogram of body weight per day. If you're regularly cycling, running, hitting the gym or working out, your protein needs go up to help promote muscle tissue growth and repair.

The general advice is that strength and endurance athletes should aim for 1.2-1.7g of protein per kilogram of bodyweight daily. So, if you weigh in at around 11 stone or 70 kg, you should be eating 84-119g of protein a day.

Protein should also be restored, which is best utilized by muscle cells when carbs are eaten with them. Quality carbs help drive amino acids from protein into the muscle cells where they are needed most. While refined sugars will do that just fine too, they will also disrupt insulin levels and are more likely to leave you fatigued not long after. Not to mention they can lead to weight gain and inflammation, which is most definitely not what you want post-workout, right?

So, now that you know what your body needs post-workout, here are 10 great plant-based options to give a try:

- **Fruit**— Fruit is a high in natural sugars, which makes it best to consume either before or right after your workout. This will allow your muscles to use the sugars from the fruit either for energy, or for restoring glycogen back in the muscle cells to aid in repair and blood sugar regulation. Their fibres will help prevent nasty drops in blood sugar later as well. Just keep in mind, you don't need a lot of fruit to get the benefits — just a piece or one serving. Fruit is healthy for us, but too much isn't necessarily more effective. Choose some berries, an apple, a banana, or perhaps some anti-inflammatory cherries, pineapple, or mango. Whatever you like!
- **Hemp protein**: Hemp protein powder is a great post-workout meal idea because though it does contain healthy fats, it's lower in fat than whole hemp seeds and higher in protein per serving. Hemp protein is generally anywhere from 4-5 grams of fat per serving and 15-16 grams of protein. It's also an anti-inflammatory protein

that's great at reducing muscle aches and fatigue thanks to the natural magnesium and iron found in hemp. Choose natural, plain hemp protein instead of sweetened options. If you don't like hemp protein, there are other comparable options like brown rice or pea protein you can try, however, no other single plant-based protein offers the complete full spectrum of nutrition benefits that hemp does. You can also find a blend of hemp, pea, and rice protein, along with some others like flax, hemp and pea, etc. Use hemp protein in a post-workout smoothie to get the best benefits, preferably with a piece of fruit to assist with complete nutrition and taste.

- **Sweet potato**: If you're up to sitting down for a meal right after you eat, choose sweet potatoes for a healthy carb source. They're rich in natural sugars but won't spike your blood sugar like refined carbs or even regular potatoes do. They also offer up trytophan, an amino acid that relaxes the body and reduces stress hormones like cortisol. Sweet potatoes are also a good source of potassium, which also helps lower stress hormones and high blood pressure. Not to mention that potassium-rich foods also restore electrolytes in the body that are often depleted right after a workout.

- ***Chia seeds*** — Chia seeds make a great post-workout addition to a smoothie because they're full of amino acids, even though not very high in protein or carbs. They're also a good source of fibre, potassium, magnesium, and iron to restore balance to the body after a workout. They can also slow down the insulin spike that might happen when you eat natural sugars such as fruit, but still allow your body to absorb them for optimal repair. Chia seeds are also great options when you're looking to lower inflammation thanks to their omega-3 fatty acids.

- ***Lentils*** — Lentils are a good source of both protein and carbs, which makes them a great post-workout meal choice. They're also fairly easy to digest for most people, which is important right after a workout for optimal absorption. (Just don't eat them before your workout — they're very high in fibre!) Try topping your sweet potato with lentils, adding them to a salad, or even adding some lentils and sweet potatoes to some broth to make a quick soup. You can also make lentil sweet potato veggie burgers as another option.

- **Green smoothie**— a green smoothie is probably one of the most popular post-workout options we have available to us today. They're amazing sources of antioxidants, fibre, anti-inflammatory chlorophyll, iron, B vitamins, magnesium, and are so easy to add protein to! Use greens like spinach, berries, chia seeds, some plant-based protein powder, and either a small piece of banana or some stevia to sweeten. Green smoothies are also easy to make in a flash when you need some quick replenishment.

- **Almonds and figs or dates**— if you like quick bites or bars after a workout, make some or buy some with a base of almonds and figs or almonds and dates. These two combinations are a wonderful blend of fibre, natural sugars, and plant-based protein. They also offer up amino acids, B vitamins, and magnesium. Add some hemp seeds to the mix, and you're really in for a delicious, nutritious (and filling) snack!
- **Spinach**— Spinach is a remarkable source of plant-based protein, iron, magnesium, and B vitamins. It makes a great green to include post-workout either in a smoothie, or with some plant-based protein and another healthy carb (like lentils and sweet potatoes) because it's filling, anti-inflammatory, and delicious! Keeping some organic spinach on hand is a great practice since you'll always have it for meals of all kinds, and to use in your post-workout regimen.

- **Oats**—if you love oats, good news — they love you right back! This is especially true after a workout when your body needs carbs and protein all at once. Oats contain not just fibre, but also other quality carbs your muscles can immediately put to use to restore energy and aid in muscle repair. If you don't eat oats, you can also try quinoa as another option. Oats and quinoa both provide quality sources of protein, with around 4-5 grams per serving, though quinoa is a complete source of protein while oats are not.
- **Pumpkin seeds**— Snacking on a few pumpkin seeds or adding them to your smoothie is a fantastic way to get in some plant-based protein, iron, and magnesium. All of these aid in repairing your muscle cells, but their high alkaline feature and high amino acid profile are what really makes pumpkin seeds so awesome. These tiny seeds reduce inflammation, keep your blood sugar stable, promote a more positive mood, and yes, keep you lean and fit too! They're also a great source of zinc to improve your immune health, which can be depleted without proper post-workout nutrition.

These are what I call "My ten green monsters" for post-workout and recovery. You can invent yours with any healthy combination of plant protein.

PROTEIN MUSCLE SYNTHESIS.

Manufacturers of sports supplements and protein powders often claim that their products can increase muscle protein synthesis (MPS). While this suggests that sports supplements somehow facilitate changes in muscle mass, the process is actually more complicated than that. Muscle growth is ultimately achieved with the combination of resistance training and protein intake.

What MPS provides us is the means to gauge how effectively those interventions work. MPS is ultimately a physiological process by which increases are linked to improved muscle growth, although the actual gains can vary from one person to the next.

Muscle protein synthesis is the process of building muscle mass. Muscle protein synthesis is essential for exercise recovery and adaptation. As such, it's a really popular topic in the fitness community. But the methods used to measure muscle protein synthesis in studies are very complicated. Some basic knowledge of the various methods is essential to draw proper conclusions from the research as you'll read.

Protein is the main building block of your muscle. Protein synthesis is the process of building new proteins. This process happens in all organs. Muscle protein synthesis is the process of building specifically muscle protein. Think of a muscle as a wall. Each brick is a protein. Muscle protein synthesis is the addition of new bricks to the wall. Now, this would mean the wall would become larger and larger. However, there is an opposing process. On the other side of the wall, a process is removing bricks. This process is called muscle protein breakdown, sometimes referred to as muscle proteolysis or muscle degradation. The speed of these two opposing processes determines the net change of the wall.

If muscle protein synthesis exceeds muscle protein breakdown, the wall will become larger (your muscles are growing). If muscle protein breakdown exceeds muscle protein synthesis, the wall is shrinking (you're losing muscle mass). The sum of these two processes determines your net balance:

Net muscle protein balance = muscle protein synthesis − muscle protein breakdown.

You can also compare it to your bank account.

balance = income − expenses

Muscle protein synthesis is the process of building muscle mass. Muscle protein breakdown is the opposing process of breaking down muscle tissue. If muscle protein synthesis exceeds muscle protein breakdown, your muscles will grow.

How Muscle Protein Synthesis Works

Protein is the building block of muscles. Muscle protein synthesis is a naturally occurring process in which protein is produced to repair muscle damage caused by intense exercise. It is an opposing force to muscle protein breakdown (MPB) in which protein is lost as a result of exercise. The ratio of MPS to MPB determines whether muscle tissues are built or lost. If MPS outpaces MPB, muscle growth is achieved. If MPB outpaces MPS, the opposite occurs.

MPS can be enhanced by increasing your protein intake immediately following exercise. The amino acids derived from protein will then be shuttled to your muscles, replacing any lost to exercise. Learning how to stimulate MPS through exercise and diet can help accelerate muscle growth, improve recovery and athletic performance, and increase overall endurance.

Effects of Exercise

Protein balance is used to describe the relationship between muscle protein breakdown and muscle protein synthesis. When your body is in protein balance, no muscle growth or wasting is occurring, and you're considered to be in a healthy state of biological equilibrium (homeostasis). To stimulate muscle growth, you essentially need to unsettle the protein balance. While it may seem counterintuitive, exercise can break down muscle protein but rarely in excess of protein synthesis. In fact, the greater the intensity of a workout, the greater the MPS.

Scientists measure intensity by something called the one-repetition maximum (1-RM), meaning the maximum weight you can lift for one repetition. According to research from the University of Nottingham, workout intensities of under 40 percent of the 1-RM will not affect MPS, whereas intensities greater than 60 percent will double or triple the MPS. Even if exercising to failure, low-intensity exercise will do little to increase MPS and, as such, will not increase muscle mass.

Effects of Diet

The relationship between diet and protein balance is less straightforward. Even with increased protein intake, MPS is triggered for only a finite period of time. This is because the body can only utilize so much of the essential amino acids (EAAs) it receives; anything more will be broken down and excreted by the liver. To stimulate MPS, it is important to consume the appropriate amount of protein following exercise. Eating too much will not improve muscle growth but may increase the accumulation of potentially harmful by-products such as urea. A study from the University of Birmingham looked into MPS response rates in men prescribed 10, 20, or 40 grams of whey protein immediately following resistance training. According to the researchers:

- A 10-gram dose of whey protein had no effect on MPS.

- A 20-gram dose increased the MPS by 49 percent.
- A 40-gram dose increased the MPS by 56 percent but also caused the excessive accumulation of urea.

Consuming 20 grams to 40 grams of whey protein after resistance training also increased concentrations of phenylalanine, leucine, and threonine, EAAs associated with lean muscle growth.

Why muscle protein breakdown is of less importance

We'll almost exclusively talk about muscle protein synthesis, and not focus much on muscle protein breakdown. That might sound like you're missing out on a whole lot, but you're not. Changes in muscle protein synthesis are much greater in response to exercise and feeding than changes in muscle protein breakdown in healthy humans.

While feeding can reduce muscle protein breakdown by approximately 50%, very little is needed to reach this maximal inhibition. This is best illustrated by a study which clamped (maintained) insulin at different concentrations and also clamped amino acids at a high concentration.

There were five conditions:

- Fasted state
- high amino acids + low insulin
- high amino acids + medium insulin
- high amino acids + high insulin
- high amino acids + very high insulin

In the illustration below, you see the effects on muscle protein breakdown.

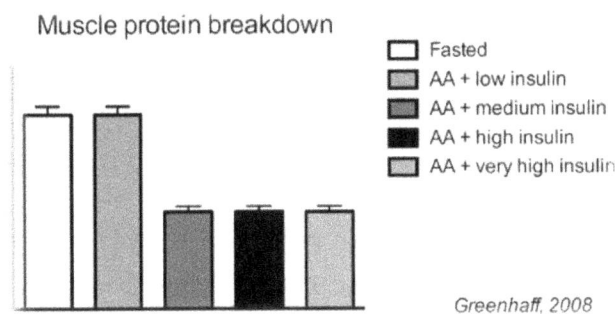

Greenhaff, 2008

In a fasted state, muscle protein breakdown rates were relatively high (condition 1). Amino acid infusion did not reduce muscle protein breakdown when insulin low (condition 2). But when insulin was infuse a moderate concentration, muscle protein breakdown rates went down (condition 3). Further increasing insulin did not have an additional effect on muscle protein breakdown (conditions 4 and 5).

This study shows us a couple of things.

Firstly, insulin inhibits muscle protein breakdown, but you only need a moderate insulin concentration to reach the maximal effect. In this study the medium insulin concentration already resulted in the maximal 50% muscle protein breakdown, but other research has shown that even half the insulin concentration of the medium group is already enough for the maximal effect.

Secondly, protein ingestion does not directly inhibit muscle protein breakdown. While protein intake can decrease muscle protein breakdown, this is because it increases the insulin concentration.

You only need a minimal amount of food to reach insulin concentrations that maximally inhibit muscle protein breakdown. In agreement, adding carbohydrates to 30 g of protein does not further decrease muscle protein breakdown rates.

Therefore, it often doesn't make much sense to measure muscle protein breakdown in nutrition studies. All study groups that got at least some amount of food will have the 50% inhibition of fasted muscle protein breakdown rates. If the effect on muscle protein breakdown is the same between groups, then changes in muscle protein net balance would be entirely be explained by differences in muscle protein synthesis.

It should be noted that HMB decreases muscle protein breakdown in an insulin independent way. It is not known of the effects of HMB and insulin on muscle protein breakdown are synergistic. However, HMB supplementation appears to have minimal effects of muscle mass gains in long-term studies.

Of course, you can speculate that muscle protein breakdown becomes more relevant during catabolic conditions during which there is significant muscle loss, such as dieting or muscle disuse (e.g. bed rest or immobilization). However, it cannot be simply assumed that the observed muscle loss in such condition is the result of increased muscle protein breakdown. After just 3 days of dieting, there is already a large decrease in muscle protein synthesis. In agreement, there is a large decrease in muscle protein synthesis during muscle disuse. Therefore, muscle loss may be largely (or even entirely) caused by a reduction in muscle protein synthesis, and not by an increase in muscle protein breakdown.

But let's say that muscle protein breakdown does go up a bit during catabolic conditions. Then the first question would be, could nutrition prevent this? If the answer is no, muscle protein breakdown is still not that relevant to measure. If nutrition does have an effect, how much would it take? Let's say you need double the amount of insulin you normally need to maximally inhibit muscle protein breakdown. That would still be a small amount of insulin that any small meal would release and all nutritional interventions have the same effect. So even during catabolic conditions, muscle protein synthesis rates are likely much more relevant than muscle protein breakdown.

While it sounds that muscle protein breakdown is a bad thing and we should try to completely prevent it, that is not necessarily true. Muscle proteins get damaged from exercise, physical activity, and metabolism (e.g. oxidative stress, inflammation etc). Muscle protein breakdown allows you to break down those damaged muscle proteins into amino acids and recycle most of them into new functional muscle proteins again.

In fact, muscle protein breakdown has beneficial roles in muscle growth and adaptation! If mice are genetically engineered so that they can't properly break down muscle protein, they are actually weaker and smaller than normal mousses. This highlights that at least some amount of muscle protein breakdown is necessary to optimally adapt to training and maximize muscle growth. So anytime you eat just about anything, you'll reduce muscle protein breakdown by 50%. We don't know how to reduce muscle protein breakdown even further, but it's not clear if we would even want that, as at least some muscle protein breakdown seems necessary for optimal muscle growth.

While muscle protein breakdown is an important process, it doesn't fluctuate much, which makes it far less important for muscle gains than muscle protein synthesis.

ENERGIZING BREAKFAST.

Vegan diets always get so much praise due to their benefits towards our health and the environment. Regardless of that, you will always run into people that are still concerned if such diets can provide all necessary nutrients. Thankfully, with the abundance of resources out there it's that much easier to find dishes suitable for all dietary needs. Look no further than these high-protein vegan breakfasts with enough plant power that will kickstart the day for you and even your non-veggie mates.

Tip: Protein content is an approximation calculated by adding the grams in the ingredients that are considered a source of protein. It is subject to change depending on optional toppings.

ORANGE FRENCH TOAST: Aquafaba is the not-so-secret ingredient that make this vegan French toast recipe soft, thick, and eggy—without the eggs. Use your favourite bread or berries to create your own signature version.

Ingredient:

1 ½ cup unsweetened, unflavoured plant milk, ½ cup almond flour, 1 cup aquafaba, 2 tablespoons pure maple syrup, ¼ teaspoon ground cinnamon, 2 pinches of salt (optional), ½ tablespoon orange zest (from half an orange), 8 whole-grain bread slices (about ¾ inches thick). 4.5 ounces (about 1 cup) blueberries or raspberries (fresh, or frozen and thawed), ½ cup applesauce, 1 teaspoon pure maple syrup.

Preparation:

Preheat the oven to 400°F. Place a wire rack over a baking sheet. Combine the plant milk, flour, aquafaba, maple syrup, cinnamon, and salt (if using) in a bowl and stir until the mixture is smooth. Transfer to a shallow pan. Stir in the orange zest and mix well. Warm a non-stick skillet over medium heat. Dip each bread slice into the mixture and let soak for a few seconds. Turnover and soak for a few seconds more. Place in the skillet and cook over medium-low heat for 2 to 3 minutes. Turn over gently, then cook the other side for 2 to 3 minutes, until golden brown. Place the toast on the wire rack and bake in the oven for 10 to 15 minutes, until crisp. Combine berries, applesauce, and maple syrup in a blender and pulse until sauce reaches a chunky consistency. Serve the French toast warm with the berry compote.

CHOCOLATE CHIP BANANA PANCAKES: These pancakes are so simple and delicious, and they're just as good for dessert as they are for breakfast! Plus, they freeze really well, so you can make an extra batch and freeze them. Use a large griddle so that you can cook three or four at a time.

Ingredient:

   1 tablespoon flaxseeds

   1¼ cups buckwheat flour

   ¼ cup old-fashioned rolled oats

   2 tablespoons unsweetened coconut flakes

   1 tablespoon baking powder

   Pinch of sea salt

   1 cup unsweetened, unflavoured plant milk

   ½ cup unsweetened applesauce

   ¼ cup pure maple syrup

   1 teaspoon pure vanilla extract

   ⅓ cup grain-sweetened, vegan mini chocolate chips

   Sliced bananas, for serving.

Preparation: Place the flaxseeds in a small saucepan with ½ cup water. Cook over medium heat until the mixture gets a little sticky and appears stringy when it drips off a spoon, 3 to 4 minutes. Immediately strain the mixture into a glass measuring cup and set aside. Discard the seeds. In a large bowl, whisk together the buckwheat flour, oats, coconut flakes, baking powder, and salt. In a medium bowl, whisk together the milk, applesauce, maple syrup, vanilla, and 2 tablespoons of the reserved flax water. Add the liquid mixture to the dry mix and stir together to blend; the batter will be thick. Stir in the chocolate chips.

Heat a non-stick griddle over medium-low heat. Pour ⅓ cup batter for each pancake onto the griddle and spread gently. Cook for 6 to 8 minutes, until the pancakes look slightly dry on top, are lightly browned on the bottom, and release easily from the pan. Flip and cook for about 5 minutes on the other side. Repeat for the remaining batter, wiping off the griddle between batches. Serve hot with sliced bananas.

BANANA ALMOND GRANOLA: This recipe was inspired by my favourite banana almond muffins. Whether in muffins or in cereal, bananas and almonds pair perfectly.

Ingredient:

  8 cups rolled oats

  2 cups pitted and chopped dates

  2 ripe bananas, peeled and chopped

  1 teaspoon almond extract

  1 teaspoon salt

  1 cup slivered almonds, toasted (optional).

Preparation: Preheat the oven to 275°F. Add the oats to a large bowl and set aside. Line two 13 × 18-inch baking sheets with parchment paper. Place the dates in a medium saucepan with 1 cup of water and bring to a boil. Cook over medium heat for 10 minutes. Add more water if needed to keep the dates from sticking to the pan. Remove from the heat and add the mixture to a blender with the bananas, almond extract, and salt. Process until smooth and creamy. Add the date mixture to the oats and mix well. Divide the granola between the two prepared baking sheets and spread out evenly. Bake for 40 to 50 minutes, stirring every 10 minutes, until the granola is crispy. Remove from the oven and let cool before adding the slivered almonds (if using). (The cereal will get even crispier as it cools.) Store the granola in an airtight container.

Chickpea Omelette: This wonderful egg-free omelette is easy to make and is good for breakfast, lunch, or dinner.

Ingredient: 1 cup chickpea flour

½ teaspoon onion powder

½ teaspoon garlic powder

¼ teaspoon white pepper

¼ teaspoon black pepper

1/3 cup nutritional yeast

½ teaspoon baking soda

3 green onions (white and green parts), chopped

4 ounces sautéed mushrooms (optional).

Preparation: Combine the chickpea flour, onion powder, garlic powder, white pepper, black pepper, nutritional yeast, and baking soda in a small bowl. Add 1 cup water and stir until the batter is smooth. Heat a frying pan over medium heat. Pour the batter into the pan, as if making pancakes. Sprinkle 1 to 2 tablespoons of the green onions and mushrooms into the batter for each omelette as it cooks. Flip the omelette. When the underside is browned, flip the omelette again, and cook the other side for a minute. Serve your amazing Chickpea Omelette topped with tomatoes, spinach, salsa, hot sauce, or whatever heart-safe, plant-perfect fixings you like.

POLENTA WITH PEARS AND CRANBERRIES: This polenta recipe is one of my favourites! For this recipe use the ripest pears you can find on the market—Bosc, Asian, or D'anjou—and fresh cranberries when they are in season (usually from October through December).

Ingredient:

1/4 cup brown rice syrup

2 pears, peeled, cored, and diced

1 cup fresh or dried cranberries

1 teaspoon ground cinnamon

1 batch Basic Polenta, kept warm

Preparation: Heat the brown rice syrup in a medium saucepan. Add the pears, cranberries, and cinnamon and cook, stirring occasionally, until the pears are tender, about 10 minutes. To serve, divide the polenta among 4 individual bowls and top with the pear compote.

FRUIT AND NUT OATMEAL: Oatmeal is one of my favourite breakfast foods. It is quick to prepare and easily adaptable to my ever-changing moods—some days I want it with fruit, some days I want it plain, and sometimes I want a little bit of everything in it (that's when I include all of the optional ingredients listed here!). This basic recipe is all you need to get started … add as much or as little of the extras as you like.

Ingredient:

¾ cup rolled oats

¼ teaspoon ground cinnamon

Pinch of sea salt

¼ cup fresh berries (optional)

½ ripe banana, sliced (optional)

2 tablespoons chopped nuts, such as walnuts, pecans, or cashews (optional)

2 tablespoons dried fruit, such as raisins, cranberries, chopped apples, chopped

Apricots (optional)

Maple syrup (optional).

Preparation: Combine the oats and 1½ cups water in a small saucepan. Bring to a boil over high heat. Reduce the heat to medium-low and cook until the water has been absorbed, about 5 minutes. Stir in the cinnamon and salt. Top with the berries, banana, nuts, and/or dried fruit, as you like. If desired, pour a little maple syrup on top. Serve hot.

EGYPTIAN BREAKFAST BEANS: This traditional Egyptian breakfast (pronounced fool mudammis) is almost always made with dried fava beans. They need to soak at least 8 hours before cooking, so start this dish the day before you want to serve it, to let the beans soak overnight. Full Medames is usually served with pita bread and a fried egg, but take some liberty and serve it over brown rice with fresh lemon instead.

Ingredient:

1½ pounds dried fava beans, soaked for 8 to 10 hours

1 medium yellow onion, peeled and diced small

4 cloves garlic, peeled and minced

1 teaspoon ground cumin

Zest and juice of 1 lemon

Sea salt

1 lemon, quartered.

Preparation: Drain and rinse the beans and add them to a large pot. Cover with 4 inches of water and bring to a boil over high heat. Reduce the heat to medium, cover, and cook until the beans are tender, 1½ to 2 hours. While the beans are cooking, sauté the onion in a medium skillet or saucepan over medium heat for 8 to 10 minutes, or until it is tender and starting to brown. Add the garlic, cumin, and lemon zest and juice and cook for 5 minutes longer. Set aside. When the beans are fully cooked, drain all but ½ cup of the liquid from the pot and add the onion mixture to the beans. Mix well and season with salt to taste. Serve garnished with the lemon quarters.

APPLE LEMON BREAKFAST: Fresh and deliciously filling, this apple-lemon breakfast bowl is beautifully flavoured with dates, cinnamon, and walnuts.

Ingredient:

4 to 5 medium apples, any variety

5 to 6 dates, pitted

Juice of 1 lemon (about 3 tablespoons)

2 tablespoons walnuts (about 6 walnut halves)

¼ teaspoon ground cinnamon.

Preparation: Core the apples and cut into large pieces. Place dates, half of the lemon juice, walnuts, cinnamon, and three quarters of the apple in the bowl of a food processor. Puree until finely ground, scraping down the sides of the bowl as needed. Add the remainder of the apples and lemon juice and pulse until the apples are shredded and the date mixture is evenly distributed.

BREAKFAST SCRAMBLE: There are many very good recipes for scrambles, but most call for tofu. In this recipe, cauliflower takes the place of the tofu—with delicious results.

Ingredient:

1 red onion, peeled and cut into ½-inch dice

1 red bell pepper, seeded and cut into ½-inch dice

1 green bell pepper, seeded and cut into ½-inch dice

2 cups sliced mushrooms (from about 8 ounces whole mushrooms)

1 large head cauliflower, cut into florets, or 2 (19-ounce) cans ackee, drained and gently rinsed

Sea salt

½ teaspoon freshly ground black pepper

1½ teaspoons turmeric

¼ teaspoon cayenne pepper, or to taste

3 cloves garlic, peeled and minced

1 to 2 tablespoons low-sodium soy sauce

¼ cup nutritional yeast (optional).

Preparation: Place the onion, red and green peppers, and mushrooms in a medium skillet or saucepan and sauté over medium-high heat for 7 to 8 minutes, or until the onion is translucent. Add water 1 to 2 tablespoons at a time to keep the vegetables from sticking to the pan. Add the cauliflower and cook for 5 to 6 minutes, or until the florets are tender. Add the salt to taste, pepper, turmeric, cayenne, garlic, soy sauce, and nutritional yeast (if using) to the pan, and cook for 5 minutes more, or until hot and fragrant.

BROWN RICE BREAKFAST PUDDING: My mom used to serve a version of this for breakfast—cooked with milk, sugar, and a hint of cinnamon. It is still one of my favourite breakfasts, although now I make a more wholesome version with almond milk and chopped dates.

Ingredient:

    3 cups cooked brown rice

    2 cups unsweetened almond milk

    1 cinnamon stick

    ⅛ to ¼ teaspoon ground cloves, to taste

    1 cup dates, pitted and chopped

    1 tart apple (such as Granny Smith), cored and chopped

    ¼ cup raisins

    Salt to taste

    ¼ cup slivered almonds, toasted.

Preparation: Combine the rice, almond milk, cinnamon stick, cloves, and dates in a medium saucepan and cook, stirring occasionally, over medium-low heat for 12 minutes, or until the mixture thickens. Remove the cinnamon stick. Add the apple, raisins, and salt and mix. Serve garnished with the toasted almonds.

CHOCOLATE BUTTERMILK PANCAKES: Everybody deserves to have a little chocolate for breakfast once in a while. These pancakes got five-star reviews from all of my testers. This recipe requires a non-stick skillet to keep the pancakes from sticking. Serve with whatever fresh fruit you like—we enjoy them with strawberries, raspberries, bananas, or a combination of all three.

Ingredient:

1¼ cups whole-grain gluten-free flour (see Notes)

2 tablespoons unsweetened cocoa powder

1 tablespoon baking powder

1 tablespoon ground flaxseed

1 tablespoon vegan mini chocolate chips (optional; see Notes)

¼ teaspoon sea salt

1 cup unsweetened, unflavoured almond milk

1 tablespoon pure maple syrup or ¼ teaspoon stevia powder

1 teaspoon vanilla extract

1 tablespoon apple cider vinegar

¼ cup unsweetened applesauce.

Preparation: Combine the dry ingredients (flour, cocoa powder, baking powder, flax, chocolate chips, and salt) in a medium bowl. Whisk until fully combined. Combine the wet ingredients (almond milk, maple syrup, vanilla, and vinegar) in a small bowl, and whisk well. This will create a vegan buttermilk for your pancakes. Add the vegan buttermilk and the applesauce to the flour mixture, and stir until the batter is just combined. Let the batter stand for 10 minutes while it rises and thickens as the flaxseeds soak; it may nearly double in size.

Heat a non-stick skillet or electric skillet griddle over medium heat and mist with a tiny bit of non-stick spray, if desired. (If you have a large skillet, you can cook multiple pancakes at once.) Scoop the batter into 3-inch rounds. Cook for 2 to 3 minutes or until the bubbles have burst in each of the pancakes and the tops start to appear dry. Flip the pancakes and cook for 1 to 2 minutes more. You should get 12 pancakes total.

BLACK BEAN AND SWEET POTATO HASH: This black bean and sweet potato hash can be an ideal breakfast, a lunch, or a light dinner. It can be served simply as a side dish, spooned over brown rice or quinoa, wrapped in a whole-wheat tortilla, or made into soft tacos garnished with avocado, cilantro, and other favourite toppings. Make it in your Instant Pot or other pressure cooker, or do it the old-fashioned way, on the stovetop.

Ingredient:

1 cup chopped onion

1 to 2 cloves garlic, minced

2 cups chopped peeled sweet potatoes (about 2 small or medium)

2 teaspoons mild or hot chili powder

⅓ cup low-sodium vegetable broth

1 cup cooked black beans

¼ cup chopped scallions

Splash of hot sauce (optional)

Chopped cilantro, for garnish.

Preparation:

Stovetop Method — Place the onions in a non-stick skillet and sauté over medium- heat, stirring occasionally, for 2 to 3 minutes. Add the garlic and stir. Add the sweet potatoes and chili powder, and stir to coat the vegetables with the chili powder. Add broth and stir. Cook for about 12 minutes more, stirring occasionally, until the potatoes are cooked through. Add more liquid 1 to 2 tablespoons at a time as needed, to keep the vegetables from sticking to the pan. Add the black beans, scallions, and salt. Cook for 1 or 2 minutes more, until the beans are heated through. Add the hot sauce (if using), and stir. Taste and adjust the seasonings. Top with chopped cilantro and serve.

***Pressure Cooker Method*—** Heat a stovetop pressure cooker over medium heat or set an electric cooker to sauté. Add the onion and cook, stirring occasionally, for 2 to 3 minutes. Add the garlic and stir. Add the sweet potatoes and chili powder. Stir to coat the sweet potatoes with the chili powder. Add the broth and stir. Lock the lid on the pressure cooker. Bring to high pressure for 3 minutes. Quick release the pressure. Remove the lid, tilting it away from you. Add the black beans, scallions, and salt. Cook for 1 or 2 minutes more over medium heat, or lock on the lid for 3 minutes, until the beans are heated through. Add the hot sauce (if using), and stir. Taste and adjust the seasonings. Top with chopped cilantro and serve.

EASY OVERNIGHT OATS WITH CHIA: To get through those busy weeks, try this easy and healthy breakfast that you can make the night before.

Ingredient:

⅔ cup gluten-free rolled oats

¼ cup plant milk

½ cup water

1 heaping tablespoon chia seeds

½-1 tablespoon maple syrup

¼ teaspoon cinnamon

Dash of vanilla bean powder or extract

Fruit of choice.

Preparation: Place oats, liquid, chia seeds, maple syrup, cinnamon, and vanilla into a 16-ounce mason jar or container of choice. Mix well. Seal shut and place jar in refrigerator overnight. In the morning, mix again and top with anything you'd like, such as fresh fruit, more chia seeds, or cacao nibs.

WHOLE-WHEAT BLUEBERRY MUFFINS: These are a perfectly delicious breakfast muffin with loads of berry goodness and a tasty, wheat backdrop. If you can find wild blueberries, use them—they are perfect for muffins because they're tiny and distribute beautifully without making the muffin soggy. If you use larger berries, like blackberries, slice them in half; otherwise they'll be too large. If you use frozen berries, bake the muffins for 26 minutes. If you use fresh, then 22 minutes should do it. Either way, check after 22 minutes to make sure you don't overbake.

Ingredient:

⅔ cup unsweetened plant-based milk

1 tablespoon ground flaxseeds

1 teaspoon apple cider vinegar

2 cups whole-wheat pastry flour

2 teaspoons baking powder

¼ teaspoon baking soda

¾ teaspoon salt

½ cup unsweetened applesauce

½ cup pure maple syrup

1½ teaspoons pure vanilla extract

1 cup berries.

Preparation: Preheat the oven to 350°F. Line a 12-cup muffin pan with silicone liners or use a non-stick or silicone muffin pan. In a large measuring cup, use a fork to vigorously mix together the plant-based milk, flaxseeds, and vinegar. Mix for about a minute, until it appears foamy. Set aside. In a medium mixing bowl, sift together the flour, baking powder, baking soda, and salt. Make a well in the centre and pour in the milk mixture. Add the applesauce, maple syrup, and vanilla to the well and stir together. Incorporate the dry ingredients into the wet ingredients until the dry ingredients are moistened (do not overmix). Fold in the berries. Fill each muffin cup three-quarters full and bake for 22 to 26 minutes, or until a knife inserted through the centre of a muffin comes out clean. Let the muffins cool completely, about 20 minutes, then carefully run a knife around the edges of each muffin to remove them from the pan.

APPLE-WALNUT BREAKFAST BREAD: Slightly sweet, oil-free, and totally satisfying, this makes a great breakfast on the run. I know you want to eat it all in one sitting (I do, too), so to avoid that calorie splurge, cut it into single servings, wrap each in plastic wrap, and put them in the freezer until needed. This also makes a great baked gift. Wrap it up, tie it with a bow—now you're everyone's favourite breakfast baker!

Ingredient:

1½ cups unsweetened applesauce
¾ cup packed light brown sugar
⅓ cup plain unsweetened almond milk or plant milk
1 tablespoon ground flax seeds mixed with 2 tablespoons warm water
2 cups all-purpose or whole wheat flour
1 teaspoon baking soda
½ teaspoon baking powder
1 teaspoon salt
1 teaspoon ground cinnamon
½ cup chopped walnuts.

Preparation: Preheat the oven to 375°F. In a large bowl, combine the applesauce, brown sugar, almond milk, and flax mixture and stir until smooth and well mixed. Set aside. In a separate bowl, combine the flour, baking soda, baking powder, salt, and cinnamon. Mix the dry ingredients into the wet ingredients just until blended. Stir in the walnuts, then transfer the batter to a 9x5-inch loaf pan, spreading evenly and smoothing the top. Bake until golden brown and a toothpick inserted in the centre comes out clean, 25 to 30 minutes. Cool in the pan for about 20 minutes, then remove from the pan and cool completely on a wire rack.

HIGH PROTEIN SALADS.

GRILLED HALLOUMI BROCCOLI SALAD: Here is a grilled halloumi salad with grilled baby broccoli, avocado and quinoa.

Ingredient: Fresh Salad

Halloumi Cheese (about 2/3 of a packet)

Half an Avocado

Baby Broccoli

Quinoa (half a cup)

Olive Oil (dressing).

Preparation: The first thing to do is to prepare your salad. Wash and dry it well. Once the halloumi is ready, you're going to want to eat it straight away as it tends to get very rubbery as it cools off so preparing everything else beforehand makes everything easier. Prepare half an avocado by slicing it into small cubes (it'll add creaminess to your salad which is why I tend to only use olive oil as my dressing).

In a pot, add some water to boil (with a pinch of salt) for the baby broccoli. I like mine fairly crunchy so 2-3 minutes was enough. Once your salad and avocado are done and your broccoli is cooking, start with your quinoa. Put half a cup of quinoa into a small pot, add about one cup of water and leave to boil (salt isn't necessary here because of the saltiness of the halloumi cheese) on a medium flame.

As your broccoli is cooking, prepare your grill pan for the halloumi cheese. On a medium flame, add a few drops of olive oil and leave it to heat up. Slice the halloumi into about centimetre thick pieces, then add to the grill pan. Your broccoli should be ready by now so add those too. For a golden-brown colour, I grilled my halloumi and broccoli for about 6 minutes, making sure to flip the cheese over to cook it evenly.

Don't forget to check on the quinoa. It should be ready once the water is gone (about 7-8 minutes), but taste to be sure (it should have a somewhat crunchy texture). Once the halloumi, broccoli, and quinoa are ready, throw everything into your salad bowl and mix well. Season with some olive oil and serve while the halloumi is hot.

BLACK BEAN LENTIL SALAD WITH LIME DRESSING:
Healthy black bean lentil salad with cumin-lime dressing! Perfect for lunches, snacks, potlucks, picnics, etc.! (Vegan, gluten-free)

Ingredient: 1 cup green/brown lentils (uncooked)

15 oz. can black beans

1 red bell pepper

1/2 small red onion

1-2 roma tomatoes

2/3 cup cilantro (stems removed)

Optional: green onion.

Juice of 1 lime

2 Tbsp. olive oil (omit for oil-free)

1 tsp. Dijon mustard

1-2 cloves garlic (minced)

1 tsp. cumin

1/2 tsp. oregano

1/8 tsp. salt

Optional: chipotle powder, chili powder, pepper, hot sauce, other seasonings, etc.

Preparation: Cook lentils according to package directions, leaving firm not mushy. Drain.

While lentils are cooking, make the dressing: place all ingredients in a small bowl and whisk to combine. Set aside. Finely dice the bell pepper, onion, and tomatoes. Roughly chop the cilantro. In a large bowl, place the black beans (rinsed and drained), bell pepper, onion, tomatoes, and lentils. Add the dressing and toss to combine. Add cilantro, and lightly toss. Serve immediately or chill covered in the fridge for at least an hour to let the flavours combine.

ARUGULA LENTIL SALAD: Arugula Lentil Salad with easy to find ingredients. It's simple, tasty, vegan and really healthy!

Ingredient: ¾ cups cashews (¾ cups = 100 g)

1 onion

3 tbsp olive oil

1 chilli / jalapeño

5-6 sun-dried tomatoes in oil

3 slices bread (whole wheat)

1 cup brown lentils, cooked (1 cup = 1 / 15oz / 400 g)

1 handful arugula/rocket (1 handful = 100 g)

1-2 tbsp balsamic vinegar

salt and pepper to taste.

Preparation: Roast the cashews on a low heat for about three minutes in a pan to maximize aroma. Then throw them into the salad bowl. Dice up and fry the onion in one third of the olive oil for about 3 minutes on a low heat. Meanwhile chop the chilli/jalapeño and dried tomatoes. Add them to the pan and fry for another 1-2 minutes. Cut the bread into big croutons. Move the onion mix into a big bowl. Now add the rest of the oil to the pan and fry the chopped-up bread until crunchy. Season with salt and pepper. Wash the arugula and add it to the bowl. Put the lentils in too, and mix them all around. Season with salt, pepper and balsamic vinegar. Serve with the croutons. Super tasty!

RED CABBAGE SALAD WITH CURRIED SEITAN: If you cook vegetarian dishes long enough, eventually you'll wind up cooking seitan. It's a "high-protein wheat gluten product" that's a staple of meatless meals.

Ingredient:

1 Tbs. olive oil

1 8-oz. pkg. seitan, cut into bite-size strips

3 cloves garlic, minced (1 Tbs.)

¾ tsp. mild curry powder

6 cups shredded red cabbage (½ small head)

1 small cucumber, sliced into thin half-moons (¾ cup)

3 green onions, thinly sliced (½ cup)

⅓ cup prepared mango chutney

⅓ cup creamy natural peanut butter.

Preparation: To make Dressing: Blend chutney, peanut butter, and 1/3 cup water in blender until smooth. Set aside. To make Salad: Heat 2 tsp. oil in large skillet over medium heat. Add seitan, and season with salt, if desired. Sauté 5 to 7 minutes, or until browned. Add garlic and remaining 1 tsp. oil, and sauté 30 seconds. Sprinkle with curry powder, and sauté 2 minutes more. Remove from heat, and keep warm. Toss cabbage and cucumber with Dressing in large bowl. Top with warm seitan and green onions.

CHICKPEA, RED KIDNEY BEAN AND FETA SALAD: rich in Protein, Fibre, anti-oxidants, and other minerals.

Ingredient:

- 1 can chickpeas
- 1 can red kidney beans
- 1 piece small of ginger grated or shredded
- 1 medium onion diced
- 2- 3 cloves garlic
- 1 tbsp olive oil
- A pinch of red chili flakes
- 3-4 spring onions green part only, chopped, scallions
- 1 cup chopped parsley OR coriander I used cilantro
- Juice of one lemon
- 150 g feta cheese – almost half cup size
- Salt and Black pepper.

Preparation: Heat 1 tablespoon of olive oil and cook the onion till lightly golden. Do not overdo it and the onions should still be crunchy. Add garlic, ginger and chili and cook till the garlic is fragrant. Set aside to cool so it doesn't melt the feta when you mix it in. Drain the chickpeas and red kidney beans, rinse and place in the salad bowl. Add crumbled feta, spring onion, parsley (or coriander) and lemon juice, season with salt and pepper. Add the cooled onion and garlic mixture and remaining oil and mix well.

THE AMAZING CHICKPEA SPINACH SALAD: These bad boy legumes are high in both fibre and protein, essential for good health and a strong digestive system.

Ingredient: 1 can chickpeas (drained and rinsed)

1 handful spinach

3.5 oz feta cheese (or similar cheese)

1 small handful raisins

½ tbsp lemon juice (white or malt vinegar is also good)

3 tsp honey

4 tbsp olive oil

0.5 - 1 tsp cumin

1 pinch salt

½ tsp chili flakes (or dried cayenne pepper will do the trick nicely).

Preparation: Chop the cheese and add with the spinach and chickpeas to a large bowl

Mix the honey, oil, lemon juice and raisins in a small bowl. Add the cumin, salt and pepper to the dressing bowl and mix well. Drizzle devilishly delicious dressing over the salad.

CURRIED CARROT SLAW WITH TEMPEH: Bold in flavour and dense in nutrition, this crunchy-nutty-sassy-savoury-sweet meal is a golden delight you will make again and again.

Ingredient: 8 ounces tempeh, sliced into triangles

1/4 tsp liquid smoke (optional)

1 1/2 Tbsp maple syrup, grade B

1 tsp extra virgin olive oil or virgin coconut oil

2-3 tsp tamari or 2 tsp soy sauce

1 Tbsp crushed raw walnuts

4 cups shredded carrots

1 small onion, diced

1 Tbsp curry powder

1/4 tsp turmeric powder (for added turmeric power, optional)

1/8 tsp black pepper

2 Tbsp tahini

1/4 cup fresh lemon juice

sweet stuff: 1 – 1 1/2 Tbsp maple syrup + an optional handful or raisins

1/2 cup flat leaf parsley, finely chopped + some for garnish

a few pinches of cayenne for heat (optional)

salt and pepper for carrot salad – to taste.

Preparation: Warm a skillet up over high heat and add in the coconut or olive oil. When oil is hot, add the tempeh triangles, tamari, maple and liquid smoke. Flip the tempeh around a bit to allow it to absorb the liquid. Cook for about 5 minutes, flipping the tempeh a few times throughout the cooking process. When tempeh is browned and edges blackened a bit, and all liquid absorbed, turn off heat. Sprinkle the walnut pieces and some black pepper over top the tempeh and set pan aside to keep triangles warm in skillet. In a large mixing bowl, add the carrots, tahini, lemon juice, spices, parsley, maple syrup, optional raisins and onion. Toss very well for a few minutes to marinate the carrots with the dressing. For a creamier salad, add another spoonful of tahini. To thin things out and make the salad zestier, add another splash of lemon juice or a teaspoon of apple cider vinegar. Finally, add salt and pepper to the carrot salad to taste. Pour the carrot salad in a large serving bowl and top with the tempeh. Serve right away or place in the fridge to serve in a few hours or up to a day later. The carrots will soften the longer they set in the fridge.

BLACK & WHITE BEAN QUINOA SALAD: This salad packs not only a protein punch but also good amounts of fibre and iron.

Ingredient:

⅓ cup (75 mL) quinoa

1 can (19 oz/540 mL) black beans, drained and rinsed

1 can (19 oz/540 mL) navy beans, drained and rinsed

1 cup (250 mL) diced cucumbers

¼ cup (50 mL) diced red onion

1 jalapeno pepper, seeded and minced (I've never used it and find the dish spicy enough for me, but feel free to add it if you like things hot!)

¼ cup (50 mL) chopped fresh coriander (cilantro)

¼ cup (50 mL) vegetable oil (I use cold pressed extra-virgin olive oil)

2 tbsp (25 mL) lime juice

1 tbsp (15 mL) cider vinegar

1 clove garlic, minced

½ tsp (2 mL) chili powder

1 tsp (5 mL) ground coriander

½ tsp (2 mL) dried oregano

¼ tsp (1 mL) salt

¼ tsp (1 mL) pepper.

Preparation: In saucepan of boiling salted ⅔ C water, cook quinoa until tender, about 12 minutes. Drain and rinse. Dressing: In large bowl, whisk together oil, lime juice, vinegar, garlic, chili powder, coriander, oregano, salt and pepper. Add quinoa, black beans, navy beans, cucumber, onion, jalapeño pepper and coriander; toss to combine.

GREEK SALAD WITH SEITAN GYROS STRIPS: You can't really mess with this classic so I have just veganised it and added some Greek style 'meat' strips and a bad ass dressing!

Ingredient: 4 tomatoes

1 punnet cherry tomatoes

1 1/2 crunchy cucumbers

1 big handful kalamata olives

1/2 Spanish onion finely sliced

1/4 stick of Cheesy mozzarella style cheese.

Fresh oregano and mint

1/4 cup good quality extra virgin olive oil

2 Tablespoons vinegar (red wine or balsamic)

1 teaspoon castor sugar

2 teaspoons mixed dried Italian herbs

1 clove finely chopped garlic

1 teaspoon soy sauce

salt

pepper.

Preparation: In a small frying pan, place gyros strips and fry until slightly blackened on the edges. Leave to cool. Cut up all your veggies roughly and place in a large bowl. Add olives, oregano, mint and chopped cheese. In a jar add all dressing ingredients. Shake well and taste. Combine the cooled gyros strips, salad and dressing and coat well.

CHICKPEA AND EDAMAME SALAD: The best part about this salad is it's so simple to whip up. It's perfect for a summer picnic with some fresh fruit, sparkling water and a warm baguette.

Ingredient: 2 15.5oz each cans chickpea (garbanzo beans) rinsed and drained

3/4 cup edamame soy beans

1/3 cup chopped red pepper

1/3 cup chopped green pepper

1/4 cup diced carrots

3 tablespoons dried cranberries

1 garlic clove minced

Dressing

2 tablespoons grapeseed oil

2 tablespoons olive oil

1 teaspoon white distilled vinegar

1 teaspoon sugar

1/4 teaspoon dried oregano

1/4 teaspoon dried basil

1/4 teaspoon dried rosemary

Salt and pepper

Preparation: In a large bowl combine chickpeas, edamame, red pepper, green pepper, carrots, dried cranberries, minced garlic and set aside. In a small bowl combine grapeseed oil, olive oil, vinegar, sugar, oregano, basil and rosemary. Whisk until blended. Pour dressing over chick peas and gently toss. Season with salt and pepper to taste. Chill for at least 30 minutes for flavours to blend. Serve chilled.

WHOLE FOOD DINNERS.

COCONUT CAULIFLOWER CURRY: Everybody loves this cauliflower curry! This easy dinner recipe is warm-spiced, nutrient packed, and ready in just over 30 minutes. Dinnertime win.

Ingredient: 1 yellow onion

1-pound sweet potato (4 cups chopped)

1 head cauliflower (5 cups chopped)

2 tablespoons olive oil

1 teaspoon kosher salt, divided

2 tablespoons curry powder*

1 tablespoon garam masala

1 teaspoon cumin

¼ teaspoon cayenne

28-ounce can dice tomatoes, San Marzano if possible

15-ounce can full-fat coconut milk

15-ounce can chickpeas

4 cups spinach leaves

Cilantro, for garnish

Brown or white rice, for serving

Preparation: Make the rice according to How to Cook White Rice, How to Cook Brown Rice, or Instant Pot Rice. Dice the onion. Chop the sweet potato into bite-sized chunks (do not peel). Chop the cauliflower into florets. Heat 2 tablespoons olive oil in a large non-stick skillet over medium-high heat. Add onion and sauté 2 minutes, then add the sweet potato and sauté 3 minutes. Add cauliflower and ½ teaspoon kosher salt and sauté another 5 minutes. Stir in 2 tablespoons curry powder, 1 tablespoon garam masala, 1 teaspoon cumin, and ¼ teaspoon cayenne. Add the Muir Glen tomatoes and coconut milk. Bring to a boil, then cover, reduce heat and simmer for about 10 minutes until the cauliflower and sweet potato are tender. Drain and rinse the chickpeas. When the vegetables are tender, add the chickpeas and 4 cups spinach and stir for 2 minutes until the spinach is wilted. Add another ½ teaspoon kosher salt to taste, adding additional salt if necessary. Garnish with chopped cilantro, and serve with brown rice.

3-BEAN HEALTHY CHILI RECIPE: This healthy chili recipe is full of good-for-you ingredients and big flavour, featuring a trio of beans, quinoa, and lots of hearty spices.

Ingredient: 3/4 cup Simply Nature Organic Quinoa

2 small or 1 medium yellow onion

3 cloves garlic

2 tablespoons olive oil

1/2 cup Simply Nature Organic Ketchup

1/4 cup chili powder

2 tablespoons dried oregano

1 tablespoon garlic powder

1 teaspoon cumin

1 cup water

3 15-ounce cans Simply Nature Organic Beans (we did 1 can each black, pinto and kidney), drained.

2 28-ounce cans Simply Nature Organic Diced Tomatoes

1 cup frozen corn

1 tablespoon yellow mustard

1 tablespoon Worcestershire sauce, vegan if desired

2 tablespoons ground Simply Nature Flax Seed (optional)

1 1/2 teaspoons kosher salt

Optional: 1 tablespoon adobo sauce (from a can of chipotle chilis).

To garnish: Sour cream or Greek yogurt (or Vegan Sour Cream or Cashew Cream for vegan), Mexican blend shredded cheese, and Southern Grove Pepitas.

Preparation: Cook the quinoa: Place the quinoa in a saucepan with 1 1/2 cups water. Bring to a boil, then reduce the heat to very low. Cover the pot, and simmer where the water is just bubbling for about 15 to 20 minutes, until the water has been completely absorbed. (Check by pulling back the quinoa with a fork to see if water remains.) Turn off the heat and let sit covered to steam for 5 minutes. Dice the onions. Mince the garlic. In a large pot or Dutch oven, heat the olive oil over medium heat. Add the onions and sauté for 5 to 7 minutes, until tender. Add the garlic and cook for 2 minutes until lightly browned. Add the ketchup and spices and cook for 1 minute until fragrant. Add all other ingredients, and throw in the quinoa whenever it is cooked. Simmer for 25 minutes. Serve immediately with toppings. Store leftovers refrigerated for up to 3 days, or frozen for 3 months.

BBQ Bean Tacos with Pineapple Salsa: These plant-based BBQ bean tacos with pineapple salsa are a delicious fast and easy dinner recipe! They're on the table in less than 30 minutes.

Ingredient: 2 15-ounce cans pinto beans

2 tablespoons Dijon mustard

1 tablespoon maple syrup

3/4 cup organic ketchup (or with natural sugars)

1/2 teaspoon garlic powder

1/2 teaspoon chili powder

3/4 teaspoon kosher salt, divided

20-ounce can (11/2 cups) pineapple chunks packed in juice* (or substitute Mango Salsa)

1/4 cup minced red onion

1/4 cup finely chopped cilantro, plus additional for garnish

1 small green cabbage

3 radishes

1 lime (wedges for squeezing)

Tortillas, for serving.

Preparation: Drain both cans of beans (no need to rinse). In a large skillet, place the beans, mustard, maple syrup, ketchup, garlic powder, chili powder, and 1/2 teaspoon kosher salt. Heat on low until thickened and warm, while making the remainder of the recipe. Drain the pineapple and finely chop it. Mince the red onion, and chop the cilantro. Mix the pineapple, red onion and cilantro together with 1/4 teaspoon kosher salt. Thinly slice the green cabbage and radishes. Slice the lime into wedges. If desired, char the tortillas by placing them on an open gas flame on medium for a few seconds per side, flipping with tongs, until they are slightly blackened and warm. To serve, place the beans in a tortilla, then add cabbage, radishes and a squeeze of lime (important, do not omit!). Top with pineapple salsa and additional cilantro if desired.

BEST WILD RICE SOUP: This wild rice soup recipe is impossibly creamy, packed with flavour and full of tender veggies and hearty rice. Everyone asks for the recipe—it's that good.

Ingredient: 1/2 cup cashews*

1 medium yellow onion

2 celery stalks

3 medium carrots

8 ounces baby Bella mushrooms

6 cloves garlic

2 tablespoons olive oil

1 tablespoon dried thyme

1 tablespoon dried oregano

8 cups vegetable broth

1 cup wild rice (not a wild rice blend)

2 teaspoons kosher salt, divided

2 15-ounce cans white beans, drained and rinsed

1/2 teaspoon black pepper

2 teaspoons dried sage

1 tablespoon soy sauce, tamari, or liquid amino.

Preparation: Place the cashews in a bowl and cover them with water. Leave them to soak while you make the recipe. Dice the onion. Thinly slice the celery. Cut the carrot into rounds. Slice the mushrooms. Mince the garlic. Add the olive oil to a Dutch oven. Add the onion, celery and carrot and cook, stirring occasionally for 5 minutes until lightly browned. Add mushrooms and sauté for 2 minutes. Add garlic, thyme and oregano and stir for 2 minutes. Add the broth, wild rice, 1 1/2 teaspoon kosher salt, and black pepper. Bring to a simmer. Simmer uncovered for 20 minutes. Then add the beans (drained and rinsed), and continue to simmer uncovered for 30 to 35 minutes more, or until rice breaks open. Using a liquid cup measure, carefully remove 2 cups of the hot soup (including broth, veggies and rice) to a blender. Add 1 cup water. Drain the cashews and add them to the blender, along with the dried sage. Blend on high for about 1 minute until creamy. Then pour the creamy mixture back into the soup. Add the soy sauce and the remaining 1/2 teaspoon kosher salt. Taste, and adjust seasonings as desired. Garnish with fresh ground pepper.

THAI SALAD WITH PEANUT SAUCE DRESSING: A fast and easy dinner recipe, this colourful Thai salad recipe features a flavourful peanut sauce dressing. It's vegan, gluten-free, and delicious!

Ingredient: 14-ounce package extra firm tofu

2 tablespoons olive oil

1/2 cup coconut milk

1/4 cup peanut butter

2 tablespoons soy

1 tablespoon lime juice

2 teaspoons honey

¼ teaspoon kosher salt

1 red pepper

1 yellow pepper

2 green onions

¼ red cabbage

4 carrots

10 ounces Earthbound Farm Organic Half & Half Baby Spinach and Spring Mix

1/4 cup crushed peanuts

Cilantro, to garnish

Lime wedges, to garnish.

Preparation: Remove the tofu from the package and blot it dry with a clean dish towel. With tofu block flat, slice it into 3 long strips, and cut the strips in half crosswise. Slice each piece into thirds. On a non-stick griddle or large skillet over low heat, warm 2 tablespoons olive oil. Place the tofu on the griddle, sprinkle with kosher salt and fresh ground pepper, and cook for 10 to 15 minutes, flipping every few minutes, until light brown and crisp on both sides. Remove from the heat and allow to cool for a few minutes, and then cut into smaller bite-sized pieces if desired. In a small bowl, whisk together coconut milk, peanut butter, soy, lime, honey, and kosher salt. Taste, and add additional peanut butter if desired (we added 1 additional tablespoon). Thinly slice the peppers, green onions and cabbage. Shred the carrots (using a julienne peeler, or us a vegetable peeler to make ribbons). To serve, place greens in a bowl. Top with vegetables and tofu and drizzle with dressing, then garnish with crushed peanuts, cilantro leaves, and a squeeze of lime.

PERFECT VEGAN BLACK BEAN BURGER: This easy vegan black bean burger is bursting with flavour: the patties are also gluten free and topped with spicy mayo & sprouts.

Ingredient: 1 small sweet potato (½ pound)

3/4 cup Bob's Red Mill gluten-free old-fashioned rolled oats

2 green onions

15-ounce can black beans

½ cup sunflower seeds (shelled)

1/2 teaspoon kosher salt

1/2 teaspoon garlic powder

2 teaspoons smoked paprika

1 ½ tablespoons soy sauce

1 ½ tablespoons mirin

4 shiitake mushrooms

1 splash each olive oil, mirin, and soy sauce

¼ cup vegan mayonnaise

2 teaspoons Sriracha hot sauce (or less to taste)

4 English muffins (gluten-free if desired, or omit)

Alfalfa sprouts, for serving.

Preparation: Preheat oven to 375°F. Wash the sweet potato and prick it with a fork. Microwave until cooked through, about 8 minutes, turning halfway through. Slice open and allow to cool until the steam dissipates and it is cool to the touch.

Place oats on cutting board and roughly chop with a knife to obtain a mixed texture. Thinly slice green onions. Drain and rinse the beans. In a bowl, combine onions, oats, beans, sunflower seeds, kosher salt, garlic powder, smoked paprika, soy sauce and mirin. Mix with your hands and lightly mash the beans with your fingers. Add ½ cup sweet potato and mix to combine. Line a baking sheet with parchment paper. Form into 4 patties and place on the baking sheet. Bake 20 minutes on one side, then flip and bake 20 minutes on the other side. Cool slightly before serving. Remove the stems and slice the shiitake mushroom caps. In a small skillet, add a splash of olive oil, mirin, and soy sauce, then sauté the mushrooms until soft, about 1 minute. Mix the mayonnaise with Sriracha. To serve, place the burgers on toasted English muffins and top with mushrooms, spicy mayo, and alfalfa sprouts.

"GET YOUR GREENS" NAAN PIZZA: This naan pizza is a quick and easy vegetarian dinner recipe, topped with hummus, kale, broccoli, and a tahini miso drizzle!

Ingredient: 1 tablespoon miso

2 tablespoons fresh orange juice

1/4 cup tahini

1/4 teaspoon ground ginger

1/4 teaspoon maple syrup or honey

1 large head broccoli, chopped into small florets (5 cups chopped)

1 bunch chard, kale, or spinach (4 cups chopped)

2 green onions

2 tablespoons olive oil

2 tablespoons soy sauce

1/2 teaspoon kosher salt

Fresh ground black pepper

7 ounces canned artichokes (1/2 14-ounce can)

2 radishes

4 naan breads (or vegan pita or flatbread)

1 cup hummus (purchased or homemade).

Preparation: Preheat the oven to 450°F. In a medium bowl, whisk the miso into the orange juice. Whisk in the tahini, ginger, and maple syrup, and 1 tablespoon water. Stir until a drizzle-able consistency is reached, adding additional water if necessary.

Chop the broccoli into small florets. Destem and chop the greens. Thinly slice the green onion. In a large skillet, heat the olive oil over medium high heat. Add the broccoli and sauté for 2 minutes. Add the chard and green onion, and cook until the chard is wilted, about 2 minutes. Add the soy sauce and 1/4 teaspoon kosher salt and sauté for another minute, until the broccoli is bright green and crisp tender. Taste, and add another 1/4 teaspoon kosher salt if desired. Roughly chop the artichoke. Slice the radish into matchsticks. Place naan directly on the oven grate and pre-bake 3 to 4 minutes per side. Remove the naan from the oven and allow to cool slightly. To serve, spread each pita with hummus. Top with greens and broccoli, artichokes, and radishes, and drizzle with the tahini miso sauce.

CHICKPEA FATTOUSH SALAD BOWL: This chickpea Fattoush salad bowl is a take on the traditional Lebanese salad; adding chickpeas makes it a filling meatless healthy dinner idea.

Ingredient: 1 garlic clove

1 large lemon (1/4 cup lemon juice plus zest)

11/2 teaspoons kosher salt, divided

1/4 teaspoon cinnamon

1/4 teaspoon allspice

11/2 teaspoons maple or honey

Fresh ground black pepper

1/2 cup plus 2 tablespoons olive oil

2 15-ounce cans chickpeas

2 teaspoons cumin

3 romaine hearts

10 ounces Village Farms heavenly Villaggio Marzano tomatoes

1 small English cucumber

2 scallions (green onions)

3 to 4 radishes

1 handful fresh mint leaves

Sumac (optional).

Preparation: Preheat the oven to 350F. Brush the pita breads on both sides with olive oil and sprinkle with a few pinches kosher salt. Slice each pita into 8 wedges with a pizza cutter. Place the wedges on a baking sheet and bake until golden and crispy, about 20 minutes.

Allow to cool slightly, then break the wedges into irregular pieces. Meanwhile, mince the garlic, then use the flat blade of your knife to scrape it into a paste. In a medium bowl whisk together the garlic, 1/4 cup lemon juice, 1/2 teaspoon kosher salt, cinnamon, allspice, maple, and several grinds of black pepper. Gradually whisk in 1/2 cup olive oil a tablespoon or two at a time until a creamy emulsion form. Drain and rinse the chickpeas, shaking off as much water as possible. In a large skillet, heat 2 tablespoons olive oil over medium heat. Add the chickpeas, cumin, 1 teaspoon kosher salt, and several grinds of black pepper and sauté for 5 minutes until the chickpeas are golden and warmed through. Chop the romaine hearts. Slice the tomatoes in half. Dice the cucumber. Thinly slice the scallions and radishes; slice the radishes in half. Thinly slice the mint leaves. To serve, place the greens in the bowl and arrange the vegetables, chickpeas, and toasted pita on top, adding a few pinches of kosher salt to the tomatoes and cucumber. Drizzle with dressing and garnish with mint and lemon zest (or sumac, if desired).

SWEET POTATOES WITH THAI PEANUT BUTTER SAUCE: These sweet potatoes topped with a zesty slaw and creamy Thai peanut butter sauce are an irresistible plant-based dinner recipe!

Ingredient: 4 medium to large sweet potatoes (10 to 12 ounces each)

    1/4 red cabbage (3 cups shredded)

    1/2 red bell pepper

    1/2 yellow bell pepper

    1 green onion

    1/4 cup chopped cilantro

    2 tablespoons fresh lime juice (1 lime)

    1/4 teaspoon kosher salt

    Crushed peanuts, for the garnish

    1/3 cup peanut butter

    2 tablespoons soy sauce

    2 tablespoons lime juice (1 lime)

    1 teaspoon maple syrup

    2 tablespoons water.

Preparation: Cook the sweet potatoes: Go to Instant Pot Sweet Potatoes or Quick Baked Sweet Potatoes. Make the slaw: Thinly slice the red cabbage, enough for 3 cups. Thinly slice the peppers. Thinly slice the green onion. Chop the cilantro. In a large bowl, mix together the cabbage, peppers, green onion and cilantro with the lime juice and kosher salt. Make the Thai peanut butter sauce: In a small bowl, whisk together the peanut butter, soy sauce, lime juice, maple syrup, and water. Taste and add a bit of kosher salt if desired (this depends on the salt content of the peanut butter). Serve: Slice the sweet potatoes in half and top them with the slaw. Drizzle with the Thai peanut butter sauce and sprinkle with chopped peanuts.

MOROCCAN STEW WITH CHICKPEAS & SWEET POTATOES: This Moroccan stew with chickpeas and sweet potatoes is an easy plant-based dinner recipe: it's incredibly flavourful featuring a blend of Moroccan spices.

Ingredient: 2 cups uncooked quinoa

   1 large onion

   3 cloves garlic

   2 large sweet potatoes (about 1 ¾ pounds)

   2 tablespoons olive oil

   1 teaspoon paprika

   1 teaspoon ground cumin

   ½ teaspoon ground coriander

   ½ teaspoon turmeric

   ½ teaspoon ground ginger

1/4 teaspoon ground cinnamon

½ teaspoon kosher salt

½ teaspoon ground black pepper

2 pinches cayenne pepper

1 15-ounce can diced tomatoes

2 cups vegetable broth

15 ounce can chickpeas, drained (or 1 1/2 cups cooked)

3 cups spinach

2 tablespoons chopped fresh cilantro, for garnish

1 lemon, for garnish

1 cup Greek yogurt, for garnish.

Preparation: Make the quinoa using the stovetop method or Instant Pot method. Dice the onion and mince 3 cloves garlic. Chop the sweet potatoes into bite-sized pieces. In a large pot, heat 2 tablespoons olive oil. Sauté the onion for about 5 minutes. Add minced garlic and sauté about 1 minute. Stir in 1 teaspoon paprika, 1 teaspoon ground cumin, ½ teaspoon ground coriander, ½ teaspoon turmeric, ½ teaspoon ground ginger, 1/4 teaspoon ground cinnamon, ½ teaspoon kosher salt, ½ teaspoon ground black pepper, and 2 pinches cayenne pepper. Stir about 30 seconds, then add diced tomatoes and 2 cups broth. Bring to a boil, then add sweet potatoes and drained and rinsed chickpeas. Simmer 25 to 30 minutes until the potatoes are tender. Stir in 3 cups spinach in the last 2 minutes. Serve garnished with chopped cilantro, fresh squeezed lemon juice, and a dollop of Greek yogurt.

SNACK AND ENERGY RECOVERY.

CHOCOLATE CHIA PUDDING: This easy and healthy chocolate chia pudding is perfect as a breakfast, snack or dessert. Vegan and naturally sweetened with dates, this is one sweet recipe you will make again and again.

Ingredient: 2 cups water

1/2 cup Brazil nuts unsalted

5 dried dates Medjool

4 mint leaves medium/large

1/2 cup chia seeds

2 tbsp cacao powder pure, unsweetened

1/2 tsp cinnamon powder

1/4 tsp sea salt iodized.

Preparation: Blend Brazil nuts, water, dates, mint and cacao in a high-speed blender until you get smooth, creamy milk.

In two clean and dry mason jars, add 1/4 cup chia seeds.

Pour Brazil nut milk equally among the two jars. Stir well and let them sit several minutes (or overnight) in the fridge, until desired consistency is reached. Serve & enjoy with fresh strawberries!

CHEESY ROASTED CHICKPEAS: Cheesy roasted chickpeas make a delicious snack or savoury topping for soups, salads, and grain bowls. You don't need to be vegan to fall in love with this plant-based recipe!

Ingredient: 1 can chickpeas, drained and rinsed

    2 tablespoons grapeseed oil

    2 tablespoons nutritional yeast

    1 teaspoon crushed rosemary

    1 teaspoon dry thyme

    1 teaspoon oregano

    1/2 teaspoon onion powder

    1/2 teaspoon garlic powder

    Salt and pepper.

Preparation: Preheat oven to 400° F and prepare a baking pan. Dry chickpeas by rolling them in between paper towel sheets or a clean kitchen towel and transfer to a large mixing bowl. Stir in grapeseed oil, nutritional yeast, crushed rosemary, thyme, oregano, onion powder, garlic powder, and salt and pepper. Spread on baking pan and place on the centre rack of oven. Cook 20 minutes, or until chickpeas are crispy and golden.

VEGAN WILD BLUEBERRY CAULIFLOWER SMOOTHIE: How about some veggies in your smoothie? Wild blueberries and purple cauliflower add brilliant colour to this breakfast.

Ingredient: ¾ cup unsweetened cashew milk

½ cup plain cashew yogurt

¾ cup frozen wild blueberries

¼ cup frozen strawberries

½ cup cauliflower florets (I used purple cauliflower), coarsely chopped

5 Tablespoons powdered peanut butter

1 teaspoon vanilla extract

2 teaspoons maple syrup.

Preparation: Blend ingredients together, and enjoy! Makes 1 smoothie.

WHITE BEAN MUFFINS (OR BARS!): These White Bean Muffins (or bars!) pack an entire can of great northern beans into a dozen muffins. They're full of protein and fibre and perfect for breakfast or snack time!

Ingredient: 1 (15 oz can) great northern beans, drained and rinsed

2 eggs

1/3 cup maple syrup

3/4 cup rolled oats

1/2 cup peanut butter (or almond butter)

1 tsp baking soda

1 tsp cinnamon

1 tsp vanilla

1/2 tsp salt

chocolate chips, craisins, shredded coconut etc for optional mix-ins.

Preparation: Combine beans, eggs and maple syrup in the food processor and blend until smooth. Add oats, peanut butter, baking soda, cinnamon, vanilla and salt and blend again. Add mix-ins, pulse a few times to mix. Pour into greased or lined muffin tins (or 9×9 pan). Add additional toppings if desired. Bake at 375 degrees for 18-20 minutes.

PANTRY CHIA SEED CRACKERS: These energizing, travel-friendly chia seed crackers are made only with pantry staples, I believe you can whip yourself something nice with what you already have of gather a few more.

Ingredient: 1/2 cup chia seeds

　1 cup water

　1/2 cup pumpkin seeds

　1/2 cup chopped pecans

　1/4 cup ground flax

　1/4 cup nutritional yeast

　1/2 teaspoon cayenne pepper optional

　salt and pepper.

Preparation: Preheat oven to 325ºF and line baking sheet with parchment. Mix chia seeds and water together and set aside to thicken. In a separate large mixing bowl, combine remaining ingredients. Stir in chia water mixture and mix until dough forms, using hands as needed. Press dough into baking sheet and roll out to about ¼" thick. Place on centre rack of oven and bake about 30 minutes. Remove baking sheet from the oven, carefully flip the dough, and then cut into squares or desired cracker shape. Spread and place the baking sheet back into the oven and bake for an additional 30 minutes or until browned and crispy. Remove from oven and allow to cool before eating. Store in an airtight container for up to a week.

VEGAN PROTEIN BARS: These Vegan Protein Bars are a wholesome, on-the-go option that provide a filling combination of protein and fibre and is a great allergy free option for those allergic to nuts, gluten or dairy.

Ingredient: 15 oz can chickpeas, drained and rinsed

½ cup oats (use gluten-free if needed)

½ cup sunflower seed butter

1/3 cup coconut sugar

1/2 tsp baking powder

1/4 tsp baking soda

½ tsp salt

1.5 tsp vanilla extract

¼ cup maple syrup (or honey if not vegan)

1/3 cup sunflower seeds

1/3 cup chocolate chips

sea salt, for sprinkling (optional).

Preparation: Preheat oven to 350. Rinse and drain chickpeas and place in ninja or food processor. Add in other ingredients and blend until smooth, adding sunflower seeds and chocolate chips in last. Spoon batter into 8x8 pan and spread evenly, sprinkling with sea salt. Bake for 25-30 minutes, or until lightly browned and set. Let cool for 10-15 minutes before eating. Bars will harden slightly upon cooling. Store cooled bars in refrigerator for up to a week.

SAVOURY HUMMUS NO BAKE ENERGY BITES: A healthy snack recipe that is full of protein and fibre, and perfect for when you are craving something savoury and want to recover some lost energy.

Ingredient:

2 cups old-fashioned oats*

1 cup Sabra Toasted Pine Nut hummus (or flavour of choice)

1 tablespoon olive oil

1/4 cup roasted chickpeas

1/4 cup sunflower seeds

1/4 cup pumpkin seeds

1/4 teaspoon salt

1/4 teaspoon pepper

1/4 teaspoon red pepper flakes

1 tablespoon nutritional yeast (optional)

seasoning blends, (optional).

Preparation: In a large bowl, stir together all ingredients until combined. Roll into 12 balls. Sprinkle or roll into seasoning blends if using. Store in an airtight container in the refrigerator for up to 4 days, or freeze for up to 3 weeks.

Maple Tahini Cashew Clusters: These maple tahini cashew clusters are a delicious snack that's easy to make with just 5 simple ingredients, but hard to stop eating! (gluten-free, vegan, refined sugar free).

Ingredient: 2 cups raw cashews

2 tbsp tahini

2 tbsp pure maple syrup

2 tsp sesame seeds

Coarse sea salt.

Preparation: Heat oven to 350°F. Line a baking sheet with parchment paper. In a bowl, Stir together cashews, tahini and maple syrup. Spread on baking sheet in close together in one large clump in a single layer. This will help it to stick into clusters instead of just single cashews. Sprinkle with sesame seeds and sea salt. Bake 20-25 min, or until golden but not burned. Remove from oven and let cool completely before breaking into clusters. Store in an airtight container on the counter.

HEALTHY EDIBLE VEGAN COOKIE DOUGH: This flour-less, vegan, low sugar "cookie dough" is full of protein and fibre thanks to the secret ingredient: beans! I assure you it has no hint of legume flavour, just guilt-free chocolatey yumminess.

Ingredient: 1 can chickpeas drained and well rinsed

.25 c sunflower seed butter can sub other nut butter if not allergic

1 tbsp lemon juice

1 tsp salt

2-3 dropper's liquid stevia or 4tbsp maple syrup

5 c allergy friendly chocolate chips.

Preparation: Add all ingredients except the chocolate chips to a food processor. Blend until smooth, stopping to scrape sides as desired. A few tablespoons of water or non-dairy milk of your choice may be needed to achieve cookie dough texture– add a bit at a time if too dry. Once fully blended, taste for desired sweetness and adjust as needed. Transfer to a medium sized bowl, add chocolate chips and mix thoroughly.

CARROT AND WHITE BEAN VEGAN BLONDIES: These healthy, vegan blondies are made with creamy peanut butter, Great Northern beans, and shredded carrots! Sneak in a few extra veggies with these gluten free treats.

Ingredient: 1/2 cup old fashioned oats – ground into a powder; be sure to get gluten free oats if needed

1/4 tsp salt

1/2 tsp baking powder

1 15.5 oz can Great Northern beans – ~1.5 cups, drained and rinsed

1/2 cup maple syrup

1 tsp vanilla extract

1/4 cup creamy peanut butter

1 cup shredded carrots – more for topping

1/4 cup chocolate chips.

Preparation: Preheat oven to 350 degrees F. Grease an 8×8 baking dish and set aside. In a high-powered blender or food processor, process/grind the old-fashioned oats into a flour. Add the salt, baking powder, Great Northern beans, maple syrup, vanilla extract, peanut butter, and shredded carrots. Blend/process at high speed for 1-2 minutes, or until you get a thick, smooth batter. You may need to stop the blender or food processor from time to time and use a rubber spatula to promote blending. Transfer the batter to the baking dish and spread it out evenly with a rubber spatula. Top with more shredded carrots and the chocolate chips. Bake for 21 to 24 minutes or until the edges of the bars get slightly brown. Remove from oven and let them sit for a few minutes before slicing them into 9 squares. Store the squares in an airtight refrigerator in the fridge for up to 5-7 days.

Conclusion.

Protein is an excellent source of fuel, nutrition and replenishment for our muscles and cells in general; whether you be an athlete or just a regular person that wants to maintain a healthy vegan diet whilst improving on every segment of your body, this guide must have helped in a way or two.

It is our sincere hope that you are able to largely benefit from all of there and become your best self; as an athlete or just a regular vegan.

www.ingramcontent.com/pod-product-compliance
Lightning Source LLC
Chambersburg PA
CBHW071810080526
44589CB00012B/744